W9-BMV-221

CANYON ROAD

CHRISTINE WHITMARSH

CONTENTS

Dedicated to my mother,
my number one fan who has always looked
upon my characters as her grandchildren.

ACKNOWLEDGMENTS

Thank you Adrian Ursu – my original Leo.

Thank you Roderick Stevens, one of my earliest creative collaborators, my DP, our house artist, and my inspiring longtime friend.

Thank you "Feisty Michelle" for your early words of encouragement, letting me know that there was something good here.

Thank you to my wise and wonderful friend Kelly for making me finish this novel that was stuck at "eighty-five percent done" for several years.

Thank you to all my book clients over the years for showing me what is possible.

Thank you to my friends and family who kept cheering for me until their throats hurt.

Thank you to Stefanie and Jessica, for your loyalty, feedback, and loving support. You are both incredible gifts in my business and my life and I am grateful for all that you do.

Finally, thank you to my husband Mike, for making me slow down and remember what it takes to write something well. Thank you for deciding to co-author this book called life with me too. And so it goes.

PROLOGUE
SINS OF THE FATHER

The old chaplain gripped his small, worn bible tightly. Only a few frayed threads and strips of brittle glue kept its spine intact. The whole thing would fall apart if he wasn't careful. He walked slowly down the cement prison block, passing cell after cell of men trapped behind bars as punishment for their sins. Each step on the cold, hard floor sent shards of hot pain shooting down the old man's legs, down to his numb feet. But he kept walking. He had resigned himself decades before to his life sentence of repentance for his own sins.

As he made his rounds on the men's block, some of the inmates looked up, nodded and acknowledged him simply with, "Father." For those, the chaplain would slide his wrinkled, contracted arthritic fingers through the bars and grasp their hands, blessing each one. Others felt too ashamed to acknowledge him. They remained in the shadows, slumping in their bunks, hiding behind newspapers and magazines. He silently blessed each one with the sign of the cross.

Some were more verbal, insulting the preacher and spitting on him. The old man didn't flinch, accepting his punishment. His eyes moved down to a dime-sized spit bubble on the right arm of his robes and for a moment, his eyes narrowed. He took a deep breath and kept walking.

"Son of a whore, son of a whore, son of a whore…" a convicted pedophile chanted rhythmically as he walked by.

The chaplain nodded at him and moved on, thinking to himself how not every son of a whore turns out to be a psycho-killer. Whores, and sons of whores, populate the world. If every son of a whore turned into a psycho-killer, there wouldn't be enough dirt to cover the bodies.

Finally, dozens of agonizing steps later, the chaplain made it over to the women's block, shuffling toward the guard booth. The staff had a standing order to page him whenever a new prisoner arrived. They told the old man it was unnecessary, especially given his physical condition, but the preacher insisted. He wanted to size up each new member of his flock immediately. In his mind, each prisoner who walked through those doors had a story that could be rewritten. For this, the chaplain was living proof.

He knocked on the guard booth door and one of the officers let him in. The men stood around the small black and white monitor watching a young woman on the screen go through the intake process. Even bundled into a baggy regulation orange jumpsuit, the chaplain could see that the girl was a pile of sticks held together by skin, her collarbones peeking out the top as a bulging female officer patted her down. The girl couldn't have been more than eighteen.

But when she pushed her thin long, scraggly blond hair out of her face, turned and looked directly into the security camera, her broken eyes and ghostly features shared her life story. The chaplain sighed deeply, in genuine sadness.

"What do you think preacher? Any hope for Lolita there?"

The guard's sarcasm was forced. He and the preacher both knew they were watching a dead woman walking.

Another chaplain might have said, "Yes, of course there's hope. There's always hope, my child."

But the old man had seen, and done, enough in life to know better. There would be no rewrite this time. For some people, life's journey from birth to death takes place on a dark, winding, and mercifully short road. This poor girl, thought the chaplain, sensing her soul through the screen, never had a chance. Grasping his rosary, the preacher crossed himself and prayed for her soul—and also her mother's. A sudden but familiar acid shot of anger began to rise in the old man's throat as he imagined the scum who destroyed this girl, probably from birth.

A person only gets one chance to be a good father. Some take their shot at fatherhood seriously and raise their kids like they're growing pieces of their own soul. Others treat their kids like the purchase of a shiny red sports car during the throes of a midlife crisis. At first it seems to calm the emotional storm. But over time, the novelty wears off and it is only the sheer guilt of the investment that makes the owner go back and play with his toy.

A bad mother can make her daughter question her own importance and her son despise women until the day he dies. The sins of the mother tend to trickle down to her daughter's self-worth and how she allows others to treat her. A bad father, however, has the power to turn his daughter into a hooker and his son into her pimp. The average prison inmate has an unlimited stash of stories explaining how the sins of his father ultimately put him behind the bars.

It was the chaplain's job to listen to the inmate victims pour out their life stories, bullshit and all, day after day. The only flaw in their thinking was that by convicting their fathers of the crimes they'd committed, they freed themselves of any responsibility. There are no get out of jail free cards, even for the sins of the father.

He left the guard booth and walked into a small room across the hall where the girl sat at a table, still handcuffed, head hanging down like a limp noodle in front of her.

A person needs a permit to carry a gun but any whore with a bun-ready oven can raise a kid.

"Bless you my child," the old man murmured, placing his hands on her head.

At his touch, the girl raised her head and looked at the preacher with a slight glimmer of hope flashing across her eyes.

Maybe there would be a rewrite after all.

CHAPTER ONE
CAESAR

It was Sunday, and like every Sunday morning, thirteen-year-old Caesar was walking the two miles to church by himself. He wore a wrinkled plaid sport coat, sweat stained white t-shirt underneath, and gray dress slacks that he'd grown out of long ago, hiked almost up to his shins. His thick, matted brownish-black hair was slicked down with water the best he could.

He walked by a narrow beige house, squeezed in between all the other narrow beige houses. There was a younger kid sitting cross-legged on the sidewalk out front playing with his Hot Wheels collection. Caesar eyed the shiny, brand new miniature cars with envy—the red Corvette, the ambulance, the vintage police car, the 18-wheeler and the holy grail of Hot Wheels—the '68 rust colored Camaro catching the sunlight in that moment. Caesar smiled salaciously at the Camaro like other boys his age looked at nudie magazines.

The kid looked up and his eyes swept up and down, taking in Caesar's appearance. He started to laugh, mocking Caesar, calling out, "Hey I know YOU! You're say-ZAR! Hey say-ZAR! Where you goin' say-ZAR?"

Caesar stopped walking, took his sport coat off, neatly folded it and hung it over his arm. Then, flashing a crooked, forced smile he walked over to the kid, standing over him and staring. The kid looked up at him curiously.

"It's pronounced CEEEEEZER, not say-ZAR," Caesar said, his dark eyes boring holes through the kid's face.

"Sorry," the kid said, shrugging and returning to his toy cars.

"Wanna give it another shot then, sport?" Caesar said, in his best *Father Knows Best* imitation from the TV reruns.

"Give what another shot?" the kid asked, looking up at Caesar with one hand shielding his eyes from the sunlight.

"Saying my name correctly," Caesar said patiently, teaching.

"What's the big deal?" the kid asked, irritated.

He looked around to see if someone more interesting might come along. The street was empty. Everyone in the burbs was either at church, watching cartoons, or asleep. The neighborhood marched to its own predictable drumbeat.

"You think names aren't a big deal?" Caesar demanded.

"It's just something you're born with," the kid said, ramming the corvette into the 18-wheeler and making crash noises.

"You are not BORN with a name! What's the matter with you?" Caesar said, trying to shove the disturbing video reels out of his mind.

"What's the matter with you? Why won't you act normal like the other kids?"

Caesar's mother's voice screamed inside his head.

At his feet, the kid was looking up at him nervously, holding the 18-wheeler in one hand, the corvette in the other.

Caesar gave him what he felt was a reassuring smile and crouched down, picking up the '68 Camaro.

"Oh I'm sorry, may I?" he asked.

"Whatever," the kid said.

"Do you want to play?" Caesar asked him.

"Aren't you a little old for this?" the kid asked.

Caesar thought of his childhood, almost completely devoid of playtime. An only child, his roles included part time cook, housekeeper, marriage mediator, and punching bag.

"I don't mind," Caesar reassured the kid.

"How about cops and robbers?" the kid suggested, grabbing the police car.

"Sure why not? I guess I'm the robber then," Caesar said.

He stood up and carefully laid his sport coat over the porch railing before returning and squatting down to keep his pants from getting dirty.

"Are you sure you want to play? You're not wearing play clothes," the kid said, getting on his hands and knees and preparing his police car for the chase.

"I only have a few minutes anyway. Besides I want to finish telling you about my name," Caesar said.

Are you serious? The kid rolled his eyes.

And then the chase was on, with the kid scrambling on his hands and knees down the front walk out toward the street pushing the police car. Caesar hunched over awkwardly, waddled comically down the pavement in his squat, guiding his Camaro in front of the police car.

"MY name was given to me by a great man, a heroic man, a man who fought for our great country and all he got in return was screwed. He named me Caesar after one of the strongest men in history, Julius Caesar, a misunderstood man," Caesar lectured.

The kid made vroom-vroom sounds with his mouth, keeping up the chase.

"Did you know that the great Julius Caesar was once kidnapped by pirates at sea and held prisoner?" Caesar continued, awkwardly scuttling down the walk like a crab.

The police car was gaining on his Camaro but he barely noticed, wrapped up in his speech.

"Well the whole time he was the pirates' prisoner, he never showed any weakness. He acted like HE was in charge! When they sent word back to shore, demanding ransom, the great Julius Caesar told them to ask for twice as much because he was insulted that they thought he was worth so little. Also, while he was their prisoner, the great Julius Caesar promised the pirates over and over that once he was free, he would have them killed. The pirates laughed at him. Laughed! Like you laughed at me earlier, underestimating me based on my appearance. And do you know what happened?"

The Hot Wheels chase reached the street and the kid stopped, looking at Caesar in surprise that he was still talking.

"Well Caesar did escape, he put together a fleet of ships and men, and chased down those pirates and then—had their throats cut," Caesar said, imitating the motion by running his index finger across his own neck.

"What's the matter with you anyway?" the kid said, standing up.

Caesar unfolded his bent legs and stood, marching in place to shake sensation back into the lower half of his body. He was no longer towering over the kid, who was about the same height.

At the other end of the walkway, the front door of the house swung open and the screen door slammed shut behind the enraged man who was now storming down the steps.

"What the hell did I say about having friends over on Sundays? It's family day, you little shithead!"

The man, wearing only his undershorts, towered over both boys. Caesar thought the kid might piss his pants right there on the spot.

"Who the hell are you?" the man demanded to Caesar, taking a threatening step toward him.

Caesar froze in place and saw his own father standing there instead, in his green army issue t-shirt and camouflage pants, bottle of Jack Daniels in one hand, cigarette in the other, drunk out of his mind and not recognizing his own son.

Nobody gives a SHIT about me! I'm a third class citizen! You and everyone else are all against me!

Caesar's stomach clenched into a tight wad of terror at the memory.

"It wasn't him, it wasn't him, it wasn't him…" Caesar started to repeat under his breath to calm himself.

"Are you some kind of mental or something?" the man in his underwear demanded of Caesar.

"I was just leaving," Caesar said, averting his eyes, quickly grabbing his sport coat from the railing, and turning around to walk away.

On the porch behind him, the man's hand made contact with his kid's face, the sound of the sharp slap echoing around the silent street. Caesar stopped, digging his fingernails into the palms of his hands. That's how he realized he was still holding the Camaro.

"C'mon you're grounded!"

Caesar turned and saw the man dragging the kid back into the house. The kid looked back at Caesar tearfully, one side of his face already developing a black and blue welt, as the front door closed in front of him.

Caesar's feet felt like anvils, weighting him down to the sidewalk. He wanted to burst into that house, and clobber the unfit father in his ugly fat face. Unfortunately, he didn't have any physical means for pulling off such a superhero feat. So instead, Caesar stood glaring at the front door, contemplating how any sort of decent God could allow such a dirt bag to be a father. Once he found that his feet could move again, he slid the toy car into his pants pocket and continued walking to church. The Camaro felt like it was burning a hole through the thin cotton, the whole way to church.

By time Caesar finally made it to the chapel, the doors were closed and services were underway. He quietly pushed the towering front doors open, wincing as they let out a mighty squeak. The narthex was empty and he was able to slip in unnoticed. He stopped at the holy water fountain, carefully laid his sport coat aside, and thrust his face directly into the golden bowl, opening his eyes fully under the water. He wished there was a full-sized version where he could strip off all his clothes and dive right in. He wanted to purify the awful images in his mind. He wanted to be reborn into a different life. Most of all, he wanted a personal guarantee from God that he would never become a man as broken as his dad. But the sinking feeling in his gut hinted that a chain of events had already been set in motion. Sliding his hands into the bowl of holy water, Caesar remembered the uncontrollable rage he'd felt standing on the sidewalk. It scared him.

Someone grabbed his shoulders, pulling him abruptly out of the water fountain, leaving him hacking up water, snorting it out of his nose and rubbing his eyes.

"Hello Caesar," Father Thomas said, smiling down at him.

"Hello Father," Caesar said bashfully, putting his sport coat back on, smoothing out his pants, and running his fingers through his hair in an attempt to flatten it.

"Running a little late this week aren't you?" the priest said, still smiling in a kindly way.

"Yes sir and I apologize for that. I had... s-some business to attend to," Caesar lied, staring down at where the father's robes touched his perfectly shined shoes.

The priest laughed.

"Oh Caesar, you're not fooling me, or the Lord our God," Father Thomas laughed. "He and I both are fully aware of your shenanigans."

"Yes Father," Caesar said.

The kindly old priest laid a hand on Caesar's shoulder and the boy looked up.

"Do you want to tell me about it?" he asked.

Caesar thought about it for a moment, and an image of the kid's terrified bruised face flashed through his head.

"Not really sir," he answered.

"That's fine my son, we should both be heading into the chapel anyway. But remember, and I know I tell you this every week...."

Caesar looked up at the priest.

"No matter what your story is today, it can be something different tomorrow. You have that choice to change it," Father Thomas told him.

"Yes Father."

"Come on son, time to repent," the priest told him, putting his arm around his shoulders and guiding him toward the chapel.

"Oh—Father, I almost forgot... I have a donation for the church," Caesar said reaching into his pocket.

He handed the rust colored Camaro to Father Thomas and instantly breathed a sigh of relief.

The priest looked at the little toy car in his hand.

"Oh and Father, you might want to drop it in the offering plate instead of giving it to the Sunday school kids to play with. Might be worth something on pawn," Caesar told him with a half smile as they entered the chapel.

Father Thomas chuckled and wagged a warning finger at Caesar as he walked down the center aisle back up to the altar where the choir was leading the congregation in a hymn.

In his sermon that day, the father preached on the topic of sexual immorality. The old women sitting around Caesar kept looking at him, as if church was suddenly a rated R event and he was supposed to be accompanied by an adult.

Caesar blushed and kept his eyes locked on his bible, reading the recommended bible verses listed in the bulletin.

As the recessional music rang out cheerfully and the outside bells clanged, Caesar processed back down the center aisle along with the other churchgoers. He had a big grin on his face and a spring to his step. For another week at least, his sinful thoughts and intentions were forgiven. The slate was once again spick and span. He was almost oblivious to the whispers of the adults about his absent parents, and the wary glances cast in his directions by his peers, who, based on the stories around town, didn't know whether to fear him or pummel him. Caesar continued out the door hanging his head and avoiding the stares, and hurried out the church back to the street.

When he got home, the strange car in the driveway gave away his mother's secret. Caesar pursed his lips together and his dark eyes narrowed as he darted through the unlocked front door. He was hit instantly by the stench of whiskey and smoldering Marlboros. A leaking cardboard container of chocolate ice cream was creating a brown liquid pool in the middle of the coffee table.

"Get me some Marlboros and ice cream!" Dad would demand.

That's how Caesar always knew he was well on his way to drunk.

At the moment, however, his father was sprawled unconscious in the recliner facing the TV, where *Apocalypse Now* was still playing on the VCR. Caesar pulled a blanket over his dad and kissed him on the forehead.

He turned his attention toward the hallway. As he moved out of the living room down the hall to his parents' bedroom and the sounds of *Apocalypse Now* faded, he could hear them—moaning, grunting; he remembered Father Thomas's words from earlier that morning about sexual immortality. He also remembered the one about honoring thy mother and father, and felt a battle ensue between his head and his heart. His throat got in the middle and he gulped down the acid.

"Whore," Caesar said, tears welling up in his eyes.

He turned right and entered his bedroom, closing the door quietly. The room looked more like an old woman's bedroom than that of a teenage boy. Religious paraphernalia mixed with dusty stacks of old books, mostly classic literature, many having to do with Ancient Rome. A narrow twin bed in the corner was draped messily with torn flowered bedding circa 1965.

"Stop it, stop it, stop it," he berated himself, angrily wiping the tears away and slamming his fists into his thighs.

Caesar faced the full-length oak mirror with a rosary draped over the top and changed out of his church clothes into a Lynyrd Skynyrd t-shirt and jeans. He looked in the mirror at the boy staring back and tried to summon the strength of a man.

"For God so loved the world."

He spit on his hands and smoothed down his hair for the tenth time that day.

"That he gave his only son."

He knelt down on the floor, slid his hand under his bed, sweeping it back and forth, and pulled out an already stuffed backpack.

"So that whoever believes in him."

Still kneeling on the floor, he slung the backpack over his shoulder.

"Shall not perish."

He got up.

"But have eternal life."

Backpack slung over his shoulder, he crossed himself reverently in the mirror on the way out his bedroom door. As soon as he entered the hallway, he was slapped in the face by the grinding sounds of his mother's adultery coming from his parents' bedroom. The explosions in the closing credits of *Apocalypse Now*, still playing in the living room, served as last minute inspiration.

Thirteen years of rage bubbled up in the boy but glancing toward the living room at his sleeping father, he took a deep calming breath and whispered to himself a reminder, "Holy mission. From God, of God."

Caesar quietly opened the bedroom door, closing it just as quietly behind him. It took a few moments before the naked couple screwing in the bed turned and noticed him standing there. The woman was far more beautiful than the man, which only angered Caesar more.

"Sinners—both of you," Caesar announced to his whore mother and her lover, an ugly balding man who dismounted and grabbed at the bed sheet to cover his fat rolls.

"You coward—more worried about your nakedness than you are about your own life, and your woman," Caesar said, still keeping his voice low, dropping the backpack.

"Caesar, get outta here, what are you doing?" his mother cried, yanking the sheet back from the fat man.

Caesar just stood there, glaring at them both.

"I'm so sorry, he's never been a normal kid," she apologized to her lover.

"You're sorry to HIM?" Caesar exclaimed.

"You stupid kid what do you want anyway?" the fat man snapped, eager to get back to screwing Caesar's mom.

Caesar's legs felt like jelly with the knowledge of what he knew God had tasked him to do. He turned and looked at the reflection of the boy in the dresser mirror and this time saw the hardened eyes of a man looking back. He reached his hand into the top dresser drawer, swept his hand back and forth and came out with his father's shiny .45 caliber semiautomatic handgun. He reached into another drawer, swept again, and brought out a fully loaded clip of shiny gold bullets (his father's childproof system, keeping them separate).

"Holy shit!" the man said, following Caesar's hands with his eyes.

Caesar slammed the clip into the bottom of the gun loudly. Then, with some effort because of the small, weak hands he'd been cursed with, he grunted as he forcefully jerked back the chamber, loading a round into it.

His mother looked at him skeptically, deep in denial that she could possibly have wrecked two whole men.

Caesar directed the gun at the piece of shit that dared lay in his father's bed, in his father's house, with his father's wife.

"Darling no!" his mother exclaimed in horror, the denial wiped clean from her sinful eyes, by utter disbelief.

She stared into the now unfamiliar face of her precious angel who went to church every week and barely ever said a word to anyone. Well—even angels sometimes turn.

"Repent woman," Caesar said in his best imitation of Father Thomas, savoring the story he'd been building in his mind for the past year, where he was the Archangel Michael, sent back to earth to enforce the Ten Commandments on a modern world full of sinners.

His mother promptly dissolved into a tearful, hyperventilating panic attack, curling up in the fetal position and grabbing her knees.

Utter weakness, Caesar thought with disgust for both pitiful creatures in the filthy bed before him.

"Now listen kid," the bald man, clearly dimwitted, said to him, in a condescending tone one takes when speaking to a misbehaving child.

"You'd better put that thing down now before someone gets hurt."

Caesar took a step forward, tightened his grip around the gun and aimed it at the center of the man's face.

"Caesar no, I'm begging you!" his mother croaked out breathlessly, gasping for air.

"Thou shalt not..." Caesar started to preach but was interrupted by signs of life in the hallway.

His mother instantly recognized her lifeline, uncurled herself and using all the breath she could muster, screamed, "JACK!" at the bedroom door.

"Oh shit," the bald man groaned, wrapped the sheet around him and fled for the bathroom. He didn't get far, stopping to puke his guts out into the toilet.

Jack, tall, scruffy, and blinking his bloodshot eyes back to consciousness, entered the bedroom and placed his hand on his son's shoulder. He was wearing a wrinkled brown jacket with the collar turned up, and a t-shirt underneath. Caesar aimed the gun at his mother.

"Jack DO something!" she screeched like a pathetic howler monkey.

"Give me the gun Caesar. This isn't your fight," said the father calmly to his son.

"Thou shalt not covet thy neighbor's wife," Caesar finished, his eyes never leaving his mother.

Her lover sat on the toilet lid, unsure of what to do and inching the door shut little by little.

"It's OK son, I've got this," Caesar's father told him, gently removing the gun from his son's sweaty, cramping hands.

His wife let out a deep sigh of relief. His wife's lover, still wrapped in the sheet, now soaked with sweat and traces of vomit, emerged cautiously from the bedroom, as if order had somehow been restored.

"Good. Now if we can all just talk about this like adults…."

BOOM.

In one smooth motion Jack raised the gun, aimed it at the bald head, splattering the man's brains right back into the bathroom.

"Arrrryyyyyeeeeaahhh," Caesar's mother screamed incoherently.

She fell off the bed to the floor and deliriously tried to scramble under the bed like a spooked cat. Jack shook his head in disgust. Caesar was still staring wide-eyed at the gory and fascinating sight in his parents' bathroom, red and white brain guts puked all over the gross, green tiled floor. He had never seen death in real life, only imagined it in his mind. The colors were much brighter and the smell more pungent than he'd imagined. He thought he recognized part of the man's eyeball lying on the counter next to his mother's hairbrush, but couldn't be sure.

Caesar was shaken out of his trance by the jarring sounds of his mother's screams from the floor next to the bed. She was still looking around desperately for an escape, screaming the whole time. Caesar thought this must be what the phrase "screaming bloody murder" meant.

"Caesar! Caesar! Sweetheart," she said crawling over to him and clutching his legs, wrapping herself around him, pleading. "Don't let this happen! I love you baby, please don't let this happen."

Caesar stared at her naked body and felt his body grow numb. He barely recognized the woman as his own mother. He felt ashamed to have come from the womb of a whore. He deserved to have been born better.

With his mother still trembling at his feet, Caesar turned and looked up into his father's eyes. He saw the bombs from *Apocalypse Now* detonating in the broken man's eyes.

"The horror… the horror."

Caesar remembered the last line of the film.

"Caesar, I want you to leave now and never come back," his father said, staring down at his wife.

Caesar nodded and it took he and his father both to untangle his mother from his legs. When they did, she collapsed on the floor, kneeling and laying her head onto the floor in defeat, sobs wracking her body.

Caesar picked up his backpack, purposefully not looking back at her.

"Son wait," Jack said, stopping the boy at the door.

He reached under his jacket collar, grabbed his dog tags, pulled them over his head and pushed them into his son's hand.

"I tried to change the ending, son. I swear to God, I tried. I just never had a chance," he told his son, tears starting to well up in his eyes.

Caesar nodded numbly. He tried desperately to extract the three words he wanted to tell his father more than anything, but couldn't push them up past the acid in his throat and out of his mouth.

"Caesar—go," his father ordered, turning his back to him.

So Caesar hurried out of the bedroom, feeling the urgent need to put as much distance as possible between himself and his father's words. If he ran fast enough, perhaps the words wouldn't touch him. They would just hang there in the bedroom, in that moment, for eternity.

Jack slammed the bedroom door shut behind Caesar.

On rubbery legs and fighting back tears, Caesar ran down the hallway, through the living room, past the Marlboros and melted ice cream, past the fuzzy gray television screen, and out the front door, closing it behind him. As his feet hit the front walk…

BOOM.

The thirteen-year-old little man ran faster, clutching his father's dog tags so tightly that they left dents in his hands. As his sneakers hit the front sidewalk…

BOOM.

He stopped and looked back at the house for an instant. The words finally made it past his throat.

"I know, Dad."

Caesar realized he was an orphan. He turned around and kept running.

CHAPTER TWO
LEO

Leo had memorized every detail of the basement including the exact number of black specks in the white ceiling tiles (578) and planks of flimsy fake wood on the walls (101) that seemed to be progressively closing in on him. His parents had locked him downstairs weeks ago, letting him upstairs only for silent meals around the family table.

Most people guessed that the small straw-haired country boy was around seven or eight on account of the ages of the kids in his class (he was actually twelve). School was a sore subject for Leo. His school experience consisted of teachers past, present and future, all screaming in unison, "Why won't you learn? Why can't you understand? What's the matter with you? Why can't you be a normal kid?" The truth was that there really was nothing wrong with Leo. But nobody believed that, including his own parents. Only Leo himself, had a strong suspicion, that he was just fine. It was the rest of the world that had everything all mixed up.

A couple years ago, Leo's parents had taken him to church for the first time. From the moment they walked through the towering doors into the giant chapel, packed row after row with people dressed in fancy clothes, Leo was mesmerized. But it wasn't the church itself, the pomp nor the circumstance, the priests in their flowing robes, the lit candles, or even the angelic voices of the choir. It was the people in the fancy clothes, the faces of the sinners who dared face God in his own house. Leo couldn't take his eyes off them. Throughout the opening procession, while everyone else watched the priest and his colorfully robed, gold-trimmed contingent march down the center aisle, Leo stared intently at a young attractive woman in a decorative blue feathery hat standing in the pew next to he and his parents. The woman started to squirm uncomfortably, glancing at Leo out of the corner of her eye.

Leo had that effect on people. While he seemed at home in most situations, other people were extremely uncomfortable around him for reasons they could never completely explain. It started as discomfort but in many cases, like this, it turned to outright anger.

After a few minutes of this she finally stopped singing and slammed down her hymnal, hissing to his parents, "What is he stupid or something?" before changing pews.

It had nothing to do with his looks either. He wasn't some kind of freak or anything like the boys who came through in the fair every year. Leo looked like an ironing board with a thick head of hair resembling a straw bathing cap, except for the fact that each strand of hair generally had its own direction. His facial features were even rectangular except for big round blue eyes that gave the impression of being continuously bewildered by everything around him.

Determined not to make yet another scene, Leo's parents ignored the angry woman in the blue hat, locking their eyes on their hymnals and singing even louder. Leo continued to stare at the woman, who moved three pews up and onto the other side of the aisle. As she did he saw her catch the eye of one of the teenage boy acolytes on the altar. The woman turned beet red and quickly returned her eyes to her hymnal.

Then, during communion, rather than bowing his head like everyone else, Leo's straw head remained snapped upright, his eyes fixated on the acolyte. Leo recognized him from school; they were the same age but the boy was a few grades ahead of him on account of Leo being held back year after year because the teachers couldn't figure out if he was actually learning anything. The acolyte returned Leo's gaze with an icy glare; Leo kept staring. The acolyte walked behind the priest down the row of worshippers, each one kneeling on the altar with hands outstretched to accept their holy wafers. Stopping at each person, the priest said a blessing, took a wafer from the silver tray the acolyte carried, and dropped it in the person's hand. Leo stared at the acolyte the whole time until, after the priest dropped him a wafer and moved on, the kid looked around quickly to make sure nobody was looking, and delivered a swift kick with his shiny black loafers to Leo's knee. Leo didn't flinch, just continued to stare, boring into the kid like a laser beam. The acolyte flashed Leo his middle finger before falling in behind the priest again.

That was the last time Leo was seen in public.

In reality, Leo knew more than people gave him credit for. He knew, just by watching and listening around school (when nobody thought he was), that the lady in the blue hat was a Sunday school teacher who had been teaching the boys in her class less about scriptures and more about the birds and the bees. This would later be revealed first through the gossip mill, and then via the local newspaper when the acolyte's parents pressed charges against the woman and the entire church. The expensive lawsuit caused the church doors to close for good, and its congregants to seek out other religions, with some using the incident as an excuse to stop going to church altogether.

"Leo come on and get a move on," his mother shouted from the top of the basement stairs.

Leo lay on his stomach in the middle of the carpeted floor. A solitary floor lamp shone a beam of light over his shoulder onto the front page of the small town newspaper, showing the Sunday school teacher, minus her blue hat, in tears, being led out of the courtroom in handcuffs. The jury was unanimous in their decision—guilty on twelve counts of child molestation. Twelve, thought Leo, just like the disciples. He couldn't wait to eventually return to church to see what else there was to learn.

"Leo I said now!" his mother shouted again.

Leo looked toward the stairs and his mother's voice, holding his breath and waiting.

"Damn it Amelia, leave the kid alone. If there's a man within twenty miles you've just gotta be on him about something, don't you?" his father's voice bellowed from above.

Leo closed the newspaper, folded it neatly and placed it on a stack of horror comics. The cover of the one on top of the stack showed a mutant reptile monster, tearing through the flesh of a barely clothed, screaming big bosomed woman. He pulled the long cord on the lamp and walked barefoot across the pitch-black basement.

When he emerged from the staircase door, his parents abruptly halted their argument as if someone had suddenly stopped a movie reel. Whatever they'd started fighting about before had come full circle to arguing over him. For a kid who didn't say much, he sure seemed to cause a lot of trouble.

Leo shuffled through the silence of the kitchen and sat quietly in his place at the dining room table. He looked up expectantly at his parents who remained standing in the kitchen staring at him anxiously, as if he might detonate at any moment.

"You called me?" he finally asked, tucking his napkin into his shirt collar.

She jerked her head to the side to look at him, her eyes slowly gaining focus. She then busied herself in the faded salmon pink kitchen, pulling a casserole out of the compact oven with peeling, pea green paint, and bringing it over to the table. Leo's father automatically took his seat at the head of the table, determined to restore normalcy to the dinnertime routine.

But the silence was far too deafening.

"It's time for dinner," Leo's mother shouted unnecessarily, slicing through the casserole with one swift stroke of her carving knife.

The two men stared at her as they helped themselves to dinner. The already frazzled looking woman with frayed salt and pepper curtains of hair hanging around her face, had reached her breaking point. She was married to a husband with no soul. And she had a son, well, a son who seemed all right, except that he was so damn impressionable. If a bird flew by the window Leo would look out at it like he had suddenly decided that becoming a bird was his life's ambition. And nothing that anyone could say or do would convince him otherwise.

When Leo was just a few months old, his mother informed the pediatrician that her son was nothing but a blank slate; a lump of clay that anybody or anything would have the power to shape or mold. She told the doctor how she wasn't so sure that Leo had the capacity to know the difference between whom or what was commanding his instincts, judgments and decisions. He was a child who blew in the direction of the strongest gust of wind. The doctor asked her how she could tell all that about a baby.

"A mother knows," she informed him with fear in her eyes.

Unfortunately, her fears had been confirmed just one week before, during the incident that had divided the three people at the dinner table and caused a cone of silence and agonizing tension to descend over their home. Leo's mother had watched it all silently from the kitchen window, washing dishes as her husband tested her son's manhood. From what she saw, Leo was failing the test. He stood sobbing over a cardboard box containing a large litter of newborn kittens. The cat he had grown up with had just given birth to them, sending his father into a violent rage. It was quite clear that the idea of additional mouths to feed was a cardinal sin for a family already struggling to put food on the table.

Leo looked up at his mother in the window as she cracked it open enough to hear his pleas for help.

"I want to come inside now," he cried out.

It wasn't so much the actual tears that earned Leo a sharp slap from the back of his father's hand to his cheek, leaving a palm-shaped welt.

"A man never looks to a woman for help!" his father scolded him.

Leo tried to reach in and pet one of the kittens but his father slapped his hand away. The kitten looked up at him with big, black saucer eyes and mewed pitifully.

"Shut up and quit stalling," Leo's father ordered him as he taped up the box, leaving a circular hole in the top.

"But they didn't do anything wrong," Leo said.

"Get the bike Leo."

Nothing.

"Get it now!"

"Daddy, no…"

Another slap and another welt.

"If you ever want to call yourself a man you will go over to that shed, grab that bike, walk your ass back over here and help me finish this," Leo's father said.

Leo looked up at his mother and stopped crying as he did. She stared at him stoically through the windowpanes, drying a dish. His mother looked out at him one more time and then disappeared from the window.

Exhausted, Leo finally gave in and did what he was told. The man and the boy worked silently for separate reasons. As they tightly sealed the hose on the top of the box with electrical tape to the exhaust pipe of the motorcycle, the mewing from inside reached fever pitch. The sounds coming from the box were no longer mews— they were the cries of a newborn baby.

In the bedroom on the other side of the small house covered in peeling piss yellow paint, Leo's mother sat on the bed, her body shaking with sobs. But as loud as she cried, the intensity of her sobs could not block out the sounds of the shrieking baby in the backyard. As the motorcycle engine revved louder and louder, her head suddenly jerked up and the tears stopped. Her eyes went dark.

At the dinner table that night those daggers were directed at the man who had first taken her innocence and then the purity of her only child.

"You killed my baby," she said.

"He's my son too," her husband said calmly before shoveling a forkful of casserole into his face.

Neither of them looked at Leo, who looked as if he was seeing his mother for the first time in his life.

"This new *thing* that you've let loose," she hissed, "is your son. My son would never have done that. He was a good boy."

Her husband stopped shoveling food long enough to deliver what he apparently thought would be the last word.

"If you don't like the way he is, I'm sure we can find a Leo-sized box to hook up to the bike tomorrow. I don't have any use for him so I'll let you make that decision as his mother," he said, swelling his chest with pride.

Within seconds, Leo was watching that same swelled chest explode all over the dinner table. His mother never left her seat. She had whipped out the handgun from under the table where she had been squeezing it tightly under her apron, between her thighs since sitting down to dinner with her family. She still didn't look at Leo but he couldn't keep his eyes off her.

"Leo," she said quietly and steadily, "I've already packed all your things into a suitcase on your bed. Go get it—and leave right now."

"Leave—where?" he asked blankly, intentionally staring away from the mangled shell slumped next to him on the table.

"Go while you still have a fighting chance at a normal life Leo," she said.

"But—" he protested, managing to stand and scramble over to his mother, putting his head on her lap.

She dropped her arms limply by her sides and stared at the ceiling, breathing rapidly.

"Do what mommy says. Go to your room Leo," she whispered, staring at the ceiling.

Leo peeled himself from the comforting warmth of his mother's lap and kissed her on the cheek. It was wet with tears. She was still staring at the ceiling. He turned before entering the hallway down to his bedroom and took one last look at his mother. She sat rigidly in her chair, now staring down the table at the shredded corpse of their torturer.

Leo had no idea where he was supposed to go from here. He thought about finding a church where he could go and be born all over again.

 **CHAPTER THREE**
TONYA

It wasn't even close to a fair fight. One scrawny, starving teenage girl was being tossed around the cement like a ragdoll by three much taller, muscly boys. She recognized at least one of her attackers but it was hard to make out the other boys in the shadow-cloaked alleyway.

As she lay on her back, regrouping for another round, a streetlight caught the face of the one she knew and he was smiling over her. She knew they weren't trying to do any serious long-term damage; they just needed to remind her of her new standing on the community social ladder.

"Is that all you've got?" he mocked. "The former queen of Shady Acres? Down for the count already?"

Tonya gritted her teeth, propped herself up on her scraped elbows and glared.

"See boys? That's the girl I was telling you about. She's a fighter!" the boy gloated to his friends.

"It's over and we both know it," Tonya said, scrambling to her feet again for another round, dukes up, eyes flashing.

"Well she'd know it wouldn't she?" one of the stranger boys laughed to the other.

"You still think I did it?" Tonya exclaimed as she sidestepped some light jabs, dancing in a circle.

They were bigger, but she was faster. It was a cat against three dinosaurs.

"Well if it wasn't you it was someone in your garbage family," one of the jabbing shadows said.

"Yeah, maybe your mother couldn't run away from all her ex-boyfriends anymore!"

"Or the goons finally came to collect their winnings from your deadbeat dad!"

The verbal blows hurt Tonya more than the physical ones and these boys knew it, especially the one who'd known her since she was little. They didn't hurt because she gave any sort of shit about her parents. No, the words were stinging reminders of the life she'd somehow accidentally been sentenced into; two useless pieces of humanity got high, united a sperm and an egg, decided to keep it, and voila—instant life sentence. For anyone else, anyway... Tonya had decided to file an appeal. Just because she was born into this, didn't mean she would die a product of it.

She continued to dance, ducking jabs from the laughing boys.

"You know you were actually a pretty cool kid—for a girl," the boy who knew her admitted. "Fellas, at one point she had the whole damn Shady Acres Trailer Park under her control. Even the adults checked with her before making any big decisions. Of course we are talking about a group of lowlifes who couldn't tell their heads from their assholes half the time, they were so high. But even still, Tonya had them all fooled. They damn near treated her like royalty!"

The boys were in near hysterics now, unable to keep up the fight in the face of this mental image of the scrawny, malnourished orphan girl with filthy greasy blonde hair ruling over a whole community. Tonya refused to let the tears well up in her eyes. She wanted all three of them dead plus anyone left in the trailer park that hadn't died in the fire.

"But then," the lead boy continued lighting up a cigarette and blowing smoke in her face, "then she let the whole thing fall apart. First dear old dad fled for the hills. Then one morning, her mom went to work at her waitressing job at the local truck stop and never came home."

Tonya stopped dancing, and stood under the alley streetlight, staring at the boy. He came over to her, standing only inches from her face. She almost threw up from the cigarette stench. He smelled like her father.

"Then what happened?" one of the other boys asked from the shadows.

He was eager to hear the rest of the soap opera that had absolutely no effect on his life whatsoever, the best kinds of tragedies.

"Then," the lead boy said, now in a softer voice, "that night, next thing any of us knew, the whole park was lit up in flames. People were screaming, little babies were screaming—remember that? 'Cuz I remember the baby screams most of all," the lead boy whispered at Tonya.

She heard the screeches playing in her head. She remembered standing outside the rec room where she'd just been playing gin rummy with old Mrs. Kenton, listening to the babies scream. And all she thought was—good, now they can run free from this place.

"I remember," she whispered.

The lead boy grinned, blew another cloud of smoke in her face and returned to his buddies, sitting down on a garbage can.

"Well I'm glad you remember that but it's too bad about the one thing you don't remember," he said.

"What's that?" his buddy said.

"The one thing the fallen queen of Shady Acres here DOESN'T seem to remember—is how that fire got set," the lead boy said, staring Tonya down.

She stood frozen in place in the middle of the alley, staring up into the streetlight. The beam of light looked like flames for a second. She turned to face the boys.

"Like I've told everyone before, and then again a hundred times after that—I don't know! I don't know!" Tonya's voice rose and she was horrified to feel the tears finally coming into her eyes.

No weakness. She choked them back, squared her shoulders and returned to face her attackers. But lounging on a building stoop over near some trashcans, they'd lost interest. They saw there was nothing else to take from her, by force or otherwise. The queen had fallen.

"C'mon, I'll show you a fire! You don't know who you're dealing with!" Tonya said, raising her fists defiantly.

The boys laughed harder than ever.

"C'mon guys, let's get outta here," the lead boy said to the others.

Then the back door of the building opened. A man dressed in a pressed black shirt and slacks, with a stiff white collar threaded-through the top of his shirt, stuck his head out the door.

"Oh there you are," he said, spotting Tonya. "You'd better come in and claim your spot. I'm about to lock the doors for the night."

"Yes Father," Tonya said, and gathered her things, a large, green army rucksack and a guitar case, and went inside.

"You know there's always space for you boys too, if you need a place to spend the night," the priest told them.

The lead boy snorted with disgust. "No offense Father, but not even if Hell itself froze over."

"Now how could I possibly take offense to that, Cameron?" the priest laughed.

"He's staying with me besides," one of the other boys said helpfully.

"Well, here's to a lifetime of generous friends. Take care of yourself, son," the father said and closed the door to the alleyway.

Inside, Tonya claimed her usual bed up by the front door and shoved her stuff under it. She didn't recognize the man lying in the bare, unmade bed next to her, studying the maze of brown water stains on the ceiling. Being the unofficial shelter ambassador (her newest "queen" role), she introduced herself.

"Hi, I'm Tonya."

Nothing.

"Did Father Mike show you where to get your bed linens?"

Silence. Tonya caught the curious gaze of a young mother she knew, who was sitting on a nearby bed brushing her toddler daughter's hair. The woman looked at the man and then back at Tonya and shrugged. The old man let out a loud hacking cough, jerking up to a sitting position to catch his breath through rasping wheezes.

"Hey are you OK? Do you need the father to call a doctor or something?" Tonya asked with concern.

The young mother covered her own mouth and her daughter's in alarm. The old man held up his index finger. Tonya waited and he soon regained his breath.

"No," he rasped, "there's nothing a doctor can do for me."

"Well do you want me to get you something to eat? Father lets me use the kitchen when I want so I could make you a bowl of soup," Tonya offered.

"Thank you young lady, but no. I just want to be left be," the old man said, laying down again and studying the ceiling.

"Look I know what that feels like too," Tonya persisted, "but you can't just give up."

"Why won't you leave me alone?" the old man asked her.

"You picked the WRONG spot buddy," a middle aged ex-hippie with a gray ponytail laughed as he walked by carrying his bed linens, "Tonya don't leave no one alone! She's the damn welcome wagon here."

Tonya flipped him the bird, then blushed when she saw the little girl notice. The young mom glared, bundled up her daughter in a blanket, and turned away from Tonya.

"Well sorry to rain on your parade young lady," the old man started, but interrupted himself with another loud cough. "But the only wagon I'm on now is the exit one. And there's nothing you or anyone else short of God can do about that."

He propped himself up on an elbow and looked at her. "Now I'm at peace with that. Why can't you be too?"

Tonya was stunned. Here she was being a perfectly good citizen, a nice person offering to help and this old man was choosing to be miserable instead. How dare he? Fuming, she went to work making up her bed, watching him out of the corner of her eye. He continued to lie on the unmade filthy mattress, without even a blanket covering him, gazing at the ceiling. She pulled her own blanket over her and laid her head on the pillow, as far from sleep as any person could be. Between the alley fight and now this, adrenaline was surging through Tonya's veins like electricity. A yell from the far end of the room disrupted her inner tirade.

"Hey now girlie? Are you gonna play for us or what?" an old woman in the corner, bundled up under several multi-colored crocheted quilts yelled out.

Yes Mrs. Kenton, Tonya thought sarcastically, remembering her cranky old gin rummy partner at Shady Acres. The old bag sat in the rec room continuously smoking Marlboros and sucking down plastic cups of cheap chardonnay from a box. When she wasn't cheating at cards with Tonya, she was memorizing the detail of every soap opera on television to later recount during the card games.

"Girl, remember how I told you Bo was cheating on Hope? What did I tell you?" Mrs. Kenton exclaimed victoriously one day, followed by, "Gin!"

By time Shady Acres burned and Tonya was left homeless, she knew more details about the fictional characters in those soap operas than she did about her own parents.

Tonya snapped back to reality, as a chorus of other regulars in the shelter chimed in.

"Yeah c'mon! Sing us a Christmas tune," another woman yelled.

"Is it Christmas?" Tonya asked.

"Who knows? When is it anything?" said the ex-hippie with the ponytail.

"Christmas…" the old man next to her suddenly said.

"Is it?" Tonya asked him.

"Nah, we missed it," he said, but then turned to look at her through bloodshot crusted over eyes. "But we could pretend."

"That's true," the young mom said hopefully, her eyes lighting up, "we could pretend and nobody could stop us. The father already locked us in and went home for the night."

Excited murmurs of, "Christmas!" quickly spread through the room. The little girl in the next bunk popped her head up and smiled hopefully at Tonya.

Tonya smiled back, got out of bed and took out her guitar, running her dry, callused fingers over the strings, carefully tuning each one. She cleared her throat. Then, she closed her eyes, opened her mouth and the silken voice of an angel emerged.

"Away in a manger, no crib for a bed…" Tonya sang, with perfect pitch.

The shelter fell instantly silently as her sweet notes filled every inch of the space.

On his bare mattress, tears spilled down the old man's face.

By the time Tonya finished her impromptu Christmas concert, everyone had fallen asleep including the old man. She quietly put her guitar away, got up and turned the lights off. She took a round-about route back to bed, stopping at the linen closet and grabbing a blanket.

"Merry Christmas," she whispered as she tucked in the old man.

She returned to her own bed, rolling onto her side and facing him, watching his chest go up and down, each crackly breath more labored than the last. Once again, she thought, God sent me someone who can't be saved. She wondered if she and Father Mike were praying to the same person. Maybe there would be a Christmas miracle, she thought, watching the man closely and willing him to live.

Somewhere between lights out and daybreak, the full moon shifted and its high beams hit Tonya right in the eye. She moaned and turned toward the curtain-less window, squinting into the light.

"Oh come onnnn…"

She went to cover her head with her pillow but noticed something was different. Something was missing.

"Oh God," she whispered, realizing that the wheezing next to her had stopped.

Other than a few quiet snores, the shelter was silent. She looked across and saw that the old man's chest wasn't rising and falling.

Tonya quickly got up and stood over him, only to see him staring right back at her, mouth gaping open. He had died mid gasp. She looked around the shelter for help, but everyone was sound asleep. With racing breaths, Tonya grabbed all her stuff and headed for the door.

"They're gonna think I did it, they're gonna blame me again," she thought frantically.

She stopped at the front door and looked back at her second dead body ever.

"Shit."

She couldn't help herself. She went back and gently covered the man's head with the blanket.

"Merry Christmas to all," she whispered toward the young mom, protecting her little girl from such a gruesome sight.

Then, grabbing the secret set of keys Father Mike told her about from under the doormat, Tonya unlocked the door from the inside and left the shelter. Standing outside in the moist predawn air, she suddenly heard a semi-truck approaching at the end of the city street.

"And to all a good night," Tonya cried out, running as fast as she could toward the 18-wheeler.

CHAPTER FOUR
CAESAR AND LEO

The prison preacher droned on in monotones that didn't match the damnation for all sinners he was predicting.

"The Lord Jesus shall be revealed from Heaven with his mighty angels in flaming fire taking vengeance on them that know not God. Sinners shall be punished with everlasting destruction," he preached rhythmically.

Sitting in the back pew, Caesar elbowed Leo with a smirk, turning his finger into a gun and mouthing, "bang bang." Leo snickered and nodded, looking proud to be in on the joke. The men around them, in the other rows of the prison chapel, kept their eyes fixed forward on the preacher, intentionally avoiding eye contact with the two unofficial mayors of the prison.

Caesar had grown into his mother's beautiful genes and charisma, combined with his father's moral convictions, multiplied in spades by his own delusions of being a vengeful arc angel sent to cleanse humanity. He was a criminal force to be reckoned with by the age of eighteen. Now, in his late thirties, he felt invincible.

Caesar looked over at Leo—part man and part scarecrow, with eerily cherubic eyes that seemed to see more than his brain could ever process. He considered this, along with Leo's eternal optimism in the face of the most awful things, his most valuable gifts as a best friend and partner in a slew of crimes.

Blinding, ugly yellow overhead lights illuminated the hot, cramped room in the minimum-security prison. Caesar knew how lucky he and Leo were to be here—considering. He thought back to when he first met his best friend in the world ten years ago.

Caesar was in a hospital restroom, washing his hands so vigorously that they were starting to turn red. Leo came out of a stall and joined him at the next sink over and started mimicking him. He worked the foam soap between his fingers and under his fingernails, rubbing harder and harder while continuously tossing glances over at Caesar. The harder Caesar scrubbed, the harder Leo did the same.

Caesar turned the water off and turned his back to Leo, walking over to the paper towel dispenser.

"What happened to your head?" Leo asked from behind him.

Caesar lifted his hand and felt the gauze bandage wrapped around his forehead. The blood was starting to dry, adhering the bandage to the jagged gash like glue.

He looked at Leo, giving him the ol' once over.

"You first. What brings you to this fine institution of mercy and medicine tonight?" he asked the gawky straw-headed man in front of him.

Leo averted his eyes as he finally turned off the steaming sink water and dried his hands.

"I was at a McDonald's having my strawberry sundae and fries, when…"

"Hold on," Caesar interrupted, "you were eating a strawberry sundae and fries? Those don't go together."

"Well, sure they do. By itself the sundae is too sweet and alone the fries are too salty, but together they're perfect," Leo said.

Caesar thought about it, nodded, and motioned for him to continue.

"I was sitting there in the bright yellow plastic booth when this lady at the counter grabs her chest and keels over. So I rushed up there and me and this other guy started pumping on her chest and blowing in her mouth because people were saying that would help. We did that until the ambulance came. Then after they got her all bundled up on the stretcher I asked if I could ride with them," Leo said.

"Hold on," Caesar interrupted again. "You got in the ambulance with a total stranger?"

"Well sure, on account of how she kind of reminded me of my mother and I haven't seen my mom in a long time so I thought it could be her. I figured I'd better go along just in case," Leo said, still unwilling to admit to himself what had really happened to his mom that day in the family dining room.

"Was it her?" Caesar asked him.

Leo looked down at his scuffed up brown boots on the pristine white tiled floor.

"Nah. Just a strange dead lady who ate too many McNuggets."

Leo looked up.

"OK your turn. What happened to your head?"

"This little scratch?" Caesar laughed, turned to leave the bathroom and looked back at Leo with mischief dancing in his eyes. "I was also enjoying a fine meal out that was rudely interrupted by a father in the next booth over, boozing it up with his whore girlfriend, swearing up a storm and generally setting a bad example for his young son. Well I went over to—educate—the gentleman about how to be a better parent, but he disagreed, with his steak knife."

Leo stared at him in awe and admiration.

"Good luck finding your mom," Caesar told Leo before leaving.

Leo hustled out the door after his new friend, his eyes wide with curiosity.

A week after that, in a desolate diner, Caesar and Leo were holding a waitress at gunpoint on the day of their first official job together. Leo kept trying to point his gun away and loosening his grip on the gun. Caesar reached over with his free hand, tightened Leo's grip and gently aimed the barrel of the gun back at the waitress. He shot a brief but significant look at Leo.

"Sorry Caesar."

The waitress behind the counter rolled her eyes, took her hands off her head and started to chew on her nails.

"Uh uh uh... Caesar didn't say take your hands off your head," Caesar said, prodding her in the side with his gun.

"I... uh..." the waitress said.

She sighed and quickly put her hands back up on her head, more annoyed then scared. But Caesar was already set off by her nonchalant attitude.

"They never obey. They NEVER obey! Leo, why don't they ever obey? Who gives a shit about loving and honoring if they never obey?" he ranted at his new partner in crime.

Unsure how to respond to Caesar's ramblings, Leo got busy, diligently gathering purses, cash and wallets, stuffing them in plastic shopping bags.

"Don't worry, we're going to pay all this back once we're back on our feet again," Leo whispered to each patron.

"Is this your correct address on your driver's license? Oh hey, March—a fellow Aries!" he said cheerfully.

He accidentally pointed his gun in a woman's face while he was studying her license.

She let out a shriek.

"Oh, sorry," Leo said, moving the gun away.

When he was done he backed toward the diner door, draping the plastic bags along his arm.

"Time to go. Time to go," Leo called out nervously to Caesar.

Caesar was still in the waitress's face as sirens began to wail in the distance.

"It's time to change your evil ways," he sang to her then looked at her name badge. "Sally.... Love, honor, and most importantly— obey. Til' death do we part."

He aimed the gun at her forehead and cocked the trigger.

She screamed and ducked behind the counter. Caesar grinned as he finally achieved the desired effect. She split her lip on the way down to the floor. Leo winced as he had a flashing glimpse of his mother, with a black eye and bloodied lip, leaning over him in bed and kissing him goodnight.

"Oh Sally, as much of a waste of nail polish and fishnet stockings as you are, there's one thing you need to know about me," Caesar told her.

"What's that?" the waitress whimpered from behind the counter.

"Leo! What's Caesar's seventh commandment?" Caesar yelled out.

"Uhhh…" Leo said, frantically searching for the answer, and then grinning as he suddenly remembered. "Oh! Thou shalt not kill, thou shalt not kill!" he said excitedly.

"That's right buddy, unless absolutely necessary," Caesar added.

Leo beamed proudly.

"Sally, we are here to offer you the chance to repent in the eyes of the Lord! To change your evil ways and become a productive member of society! Do you think you can do that for me Sally? Do you think you can be more than a walking and talking social security number, a pink polyester vagina waiting to poison some unlucky man's world?" Caesar raged, feeling the demons of his past bubbling up in his throat, threatening to overtake him.

Like a dog understanding only his master's tone of words, but not the words themselves, Sally began to shriek in terror. Leo froze in the doorway, staring at his new partner with wide eyes.

Caesar looked over at him and quickly recovered, laughing.

"Not to worry buddy. Everything's under control," he told him.

The two fled out the door to the parking lot into Caesar's borrowed yellow Ford Mustang and sped away in a cloud of dust.

From that day on, the two embarked on a "humanity cleansing" mission across America. This meant identifying problematic members of society, and punishing them in one way or another to send a message. Guys with resumes as impressive as theirs, were usually sent directly to super maximum security Pelican Bay State Prison.

However, a combination of bureaucratic bullshit, an inexperienced district attorney, and the fact that most of the "cleansing" equated to little more than preaching, pranks, and petty theft, got them a lesser sentence. There was also the jury packed with sympathetic housewives who wanted nothing more than to mother poor, misguided orphan Leo and screw charismatic, handsome, youthful-looking Caesar.

Caesar preferred to think of their current residence as a veritable desert resort for independent-minded men who strayed a few yards too far from the sheep herd. Plus, he reasoned, when white-collar guys did what he and Leo had done, just without shopping bags and guns, they got the same resort treatment, sometimes even better. He didn't even mind the constant head shrinking and daily dose of religion, which fed his lifelong passion for learning new things. Overall, he saw the whole experience as an opportunity to improve his life.

Caesar looked up at the preacher, listening to tales of God raining down wrath and fury on those who crossed him. Caesar frowned and shook his head.

"I'm tellin' you Leo, no self-respecting father would ever do that kinda shit to his kids," Caesar said.

"Are you sure?" Leo asked, turning to give Caesar his undivided attention.

"What do you mean, are you sure? What kind of father do you know that would send his kids to Hell for eternity?" Caesar snapped.

"Some, maybe…" Leo said.

The preacher finished his sermon and ended the service.

"In the name of the Father, Son…"

An inmate in the front row finished for him.

"And holy stinkin' spirit! Wrap it up preacher!" the inmate shouted, triggering ripples of snickering throughout the room.

"Amen!" Caesar and Leo said, grinning at each other.

"Settle down ladies," one of the many guards in the room shouted.

The room settled long enough for an orderly dismissal, rows of men in orange jumpsuits filing past bored looking guards with clubs and Taser guns.

"Lights out in ten minutes," a voice from overhead announced as the guard led Caesar and Leo and the other inmates from their block, down the center aisle toward their cell.

Caesar strode down the row of cells to the end, exchanging nods, waves and greetings with his citizens. But tonight his mind was elsewhere. Leo tagged along behind him, keeping his head down.

As they arrived at their cell the door slid open by the unseen electronic eyes of the booth guard. The guard turned to his trainee sitting next to him.

"You know, if you learn to read what the inmates have written on their walls, you see it's a picture into their minds," he told the young clean-shaven guy.

"Is that a fact? What about the mayor there and his lieutenant," the trainee said, pointing out Caesar and Leo on the cheap black and white video monitors as they entered their cell.

The booth guard smirked.

"Those two? You've gotta see it to believe it."

Caesar and Leo walked into their cell. The square cement box was decorated with various Christian religious paraphernalia—crosses, crucifixes and pictures of Jesus on the walls and bible passages scratched into the concrete. In stark contrast yet mixed in seamlessly with the religious decorations, were Playboy centerfolds with oily fingerprint marks, and newspaper clippings of notorious criminals who had, even for a short time, been successful in their crime endeavors. The cell had two sets of bunk beds but only one set was occupied.

Leo climbed up into the top bunk and lay there staring at the ceiling. Caesar sat down on his lower bunk. He reached into his pillowcase and pulled out a crumpled envelope. Caesar carefully slid a photo out and looked at the woman's pregnant belly in the picture.

"Who's that?" Leo asked.

Caesar hadn't even heard him shift in the bunk above. Now his straw head was hanging upside down in space staring at the photo in Caesar's lap.

"This," Caesar proclaimed, "is our new life."

He passed the photo of Loretta's belly up to Leo.

"Lights out!" the loudspeaker boomed.

Darkness enveloped the cell and Leo passed the photo back down again.

"Our new... I don't get it," Leo said.

"My baby lives in that belly. I think that's why Loretta hasn't called or written since sending that picture to me. She's testing me to make sure I'm fit to be our baby's daddy. It's my job to prove that I am," Caesar said.

"That's really smart because not everyone should be someone's daddy," Leo said.

"Damn right they shouldn't. But personally I think I was put on this earth to be one. I spent a lot of time watching my father when I was little. He was a pretty good example—most of the time," Caesar said, trailing off.

He visualized in one rapid-fire film reel, all the good times he had when his father was sober. His favorites were the unofficial "bring your kid to work" days when his father yanked Caesar out of school (without telling his mother) and took him on the road with him in his big rig. Caesar often fantasized about bringing his own son to work with him someday; the pride he'd feel.

Don't do it that way son, do it this way instead.

He imagined himself teaching his boy with pride. He wondered what he'd be doing for a living by then.

"I think you'll be a great daddy. You've been great so far," said Leo.

"So you're in?" Caesar lowered his voice to a whisper.

"I'm in what?" asked Leo.

"In with me to go to Loretta and help raise our kid. You can be the baby's godfather," Caesar whispered.

The long silence from above made Caesar nervous. But then when he heard sniffles coming from Leo's bunk he understood.

"Well jeez, you don't have to get all weepy about it," he muttered, his insides twitching.

"I just can't believe... you'd ask me..." Leo sniffled.

"You're a good person Leo. The best person I know," Caesar said.

"Thank you Caesar. You're the best person I know too," Leo sniffled.

Twenty-four hours later, Caesar was viciously slamming the bloodied, beaten head of another inmate into the unforgiving steel of the cell toilet. The man occasionally grunted and tried to resist, but that only made the beating worse. Caesar said nothing as he took care of business with a steely, calm resolve, not letting his emotions get the best of him. This was nothing but a housekeeping task.

Leo lay on the top bunk looking down on the scene over a magazine he was pretending to read.

"I-told-them-we-didn't-need-a-roommate," he sang quietly to himself.

He turned to face the wall, putting his back to Caesar as his friend continued to give their new roommate the beating of his life.

"Filthy, kid rapist," Caesar yelled as he punched and kicked the man unconscious into the corner.

At the other end of the block, the booth guard and his trainee played cards and drank coffee from Styrofoam cups in their sturdy glass booth, looking vaguely interested in the typical goings on of the block playing out on the monitors. The black and white monitors with frequently freezing images had the tendency of making current events look more like old newsreels. The slow motion silent films made it hard to tell what was actually happening now versus instant replay."

The trainee pointed out the flickering image on the screen of Caesar bashing his new cellmate's head against the metal toilet seat as if trying to break open a coconut.

His boss peered at the wavy lines of static now distorting the image and hit the top of the monitor with his fist. He looked at it for a moment before returning to his hand of cards.

"Good. Let the mayor teach the pedophile a lesson. Saves us the trouble," he said, with a half-hearted smirk.

"Pedophile? I didn't think we had ones that serious in here? Isn't he in for unpaid traffic tickets?" the trainee asked.

"Kid one thing you're going to learn here is that nothing is as it seems. Do you think those two," he said indicating Caesar and Leo, "are really in here for petty theft?"

The guards returned to their game as, on the video monitor, Caesar stepped away from the crumpled form of the beaten inmate in the corner of the cell.

He strode confidently over to the cell bars, preaching loudly out to his block. Arms snaked their way through every set of bars, followed by faces pressed eagerly up against them, hanging on to Caesar's every word.

"My children, God has given ME the REAL word. Are we to believe that the same doctrine allegedly handed down to one man on a mountaintop, thousands of years ago is still the true gospel of the Lord?" he announced to the cellblock.

The inmates chimed in with their agreement.

"You're damn right no! Times have changed my children! People have changed and what was once the truth is now a lie, sold to the ignorant masses by those who wish to control them. We are in a world where we MUST covet, forsake, and murder those who deserve it, for the greater good and survival of society! When they tell us we are wrong, they are making us weak—puppets to be controlled for purposes of TRUE evil!" Caesar continued.

He paused for dramatic effect. Leo stood at attention behind him, his ever-ready deputy.

"So my children... for the purpose of survival and well being..."

The noise level suddenly doubled.

Back in the booth, the booth guard rolled his eyes at his wide-eyed trainee and laid down three aces.

"Oh Lordie, there he goes again," he sighed.

"Should we do something?" the trainee asked, readying his duty weapon.

"Easy there kid; around here this is just what we call Tuesday," the older man laughed. "I've known this guy for years. In a strange way I think he's even on our side. He hates the bad guys more than we do. Look at what he did to the kid fucker we put in there with him. Takes some balls, sacrificing yourself to go after scum."

"Sir, I might be out of line, but it sounds like you're apologizing for the guy," the trainee said cautiously.

"Son, don't venture to tell me what I am or am not doing or thinking about any of these guys. One thing I've learned on this job after twenty plus years, is that the reason that men do things are never as straightforward as people make 'em out to be. The human mind and soul don't work that way."

The trainee kept his eyes on his cards and didn't say a word. The older man glanced at the monitor, sighed, and looked away.

"When you take away a natural-born warrior's dignity... he almost always finds a way to get it back," he said.

Back in the cell, Caesar jumped off the toilet seat and leaned against the cell bars, gripping them with power. In his world, he was infallible. The prison lights shone on him with focused brilliance.

"To heal society in the elimination of true evil, I have been blessed by God with a NEW set of commandments!" he said.

Everything magnified to its fullest potential. The lights glared, the inmates roared, and an invisible choir of heavenly singers rejoiced from behind Caesar as Leo conducted them. Caesar looked down and saw that he was levitating inches from the ground. Behind him, Leo was quickly gathering their few meager belongings and stuffing them in a pillowcase. The big finale was almost over and the curtain was about to fall.

"Caesar's commandment number one—do the job one hundred percent or don't bother doing it at all," Caesar roared on.

Leo joined him at his side, watching as Caesar floated gently back to the floor. He held one hand over his eyes, as the lights grew even brighter and started sweeping the cellblock.

"Because if you don't, some dummy will always come along who can do it better. Commandment number two—never swear in front of kids. They're innocent; they don't need to hear about your shit," he continued.

"Hell no!" yelled one of his disciples hanging through the bars of his cell.

"Tell us preacher!" another one yelled.

The cell bars vibrated under Caesar's hands. The vibrations spread quickly down the entire block and all the bars vibrated in unison. Leo picked up the pillowcase and stepped forward expectantly. Caesar shouted even louder to make himself heard over the chaos.

"Do you have it?"

"What?" Leo shouted.

"Do you have it?" Caesar shouted louder.

Leo nodded and quickly produced the crumpled photo from the bag and showed Caesar, who grabbed the belly photo and shoved it in his jumpsuit pocket.

"So we're still doing this?" Leo asked pointlessly.

"What did you think?" Caesar asked.

"You know, Jesus didn't have any kids as far as I know," said Leo.

"Good to know," Caesar said.

Back in the booth, the trainee looked up from his cards at the monitor. Under the cover of flickering, shorting out yellow lights, Caesar yelled maniacally through his cell bars to the other inmates. Some blatantly ignored him while others shoved rude hand gestures through the bars.

"Shut up freak!" an inmate yelled in real time.

"Give it a rest will ya?" another one demanded.

The lights flickered and made a buzzing sound, then returned to normal.

In Caesar's world though, the vibrating doors on all the cells slid aside and the doors opened. Inmates rushed out of their cells to line the cellblock aisle in reverent celebration. Caesar stepped grandiosely out of his cell with Leo trailing behind, ensuring that their fellow inmates bestowed the proper respect.

"And commandment number three—once you make your choice and commit to it, never go back," he roared triumphantly.

The inmates dropped to their knees, bowing deeply as Caesar and Leo marched triumphantly up the corridor to the guard booth, where both guards emerged, blocking their way. Caesar and Leo stopped.

"Caesar," the older booth guard said, sounding in awe of the word.

He thrust his hand forward, grabbing Caesar's and pumped it heartily as tears welled up in his eyes.

"It sure has been a pleasure knowing you. You are one of the strongest, surest men I've ever met," he said.

The trainee followed suit.

"Same here Caesar. I was wrong before about thinking you were a bad man," the tearful young man said.

"And thank YOU both for believing in the truth," Caesar said, making the sign of the cross over their heads.

"We have to be going now," Leo said.

Both guards removed their guns from the holsters and handed them to Caesar and Leo.

""We sure will miss you," the older guard said.

The two guards scurried back into the booth, dropped to their knees and faced the wall.

"We sure are two lucky bastards to have been saved like this," one said to the other, sharing a vacuous smile.

Caesar aimed his new gun and fired into the back of the booth guard's head.

"Yes you are," he said.

Leo did the same for the trainee, leaning forward slightly to see what he had done.

"Like that?" he asked for Caesar's approval.

Caesar inspected Leo's work.

"Getting better every time buddy," Caesar said approvingly.

Leo grinned.

Meanwhile in the real world, events were far less dramatic. Having done their allotted time, Caesar and Leo checked out of prison with the matter-of-fact processing of two travelers checking out of a Holiday Inn. They were dressed in dirty t-shirts, jeans and cloth sneakers with holes in them. Each man signed for his own possessions. The guard in the steel cage slid a large padded yellow envelope across the counter like a casino cashier. Caesar immediately opened the envelope, fished out his father's dog tags and put them around his neck, breathing a sigh of relief.

"Ready?" Caesar asked Leo.

"Yeah Caesar," Leo said smiling.

The two were escorted down a long, silent concrete hallway right out of the prison. Out the door, across the dirt yard and the bored-looking guards never said a word; nothing out of the ordinary here. The dull silence of their exit was deafening to Caesar, so he let his mind wander again.

Under the glare of spotlights like a Hollywood premiere, the main gates parted as Caesar and Leo emerged, pumping their fists in the air victoriously. The gates closed behind them, cloaking them in darkness and a moment of silence.

"Now what?" Leo asked.

"Now, we free the chosen one," Caesar said dramatically and the crowd behind the gates cheered triumphantly for their warrior.

But as soon as Caesar turned away from the gates and looked out into the baking hot desert, the scene changed again. The gates behind them slid slowly shut with a screeching clank. Caesar and Leo looked at each other, shrugged and strolled off down the road.

"Now what?" asked Leo.

"Ask me again tomorrow," Caesar said uncertainly, the delusions of grandeur temporarily discarded on the side of the dusty highway.

CHAPTER FIVE
CONFESSION

Far off the beaten path from the prison, a lanky teenage boy dozed in a lawn chair in front of a shack of a gas station. The sunlight shining on the boy was suddenly blocked out by two shadows looming over him. He continued to snore.

Caesar and Leo, in their dust-covered, sweat-soaked clothes, looked around grimly.

"No wheels," said Caesar.

He went inside the gas station and rummaged around. Leo stood guard in front of the sleeping teenager who continued to snore. Caesar reemerged with a battered old .45 handgun that reminded him of his dad's gun, yanking at the rusty chamber to get it to slide open. He blew into the dusty chamber.

"Disgusting. Doesn't have enough common decency and respect to maintain his weapon," he muttered.

"Wonder what he uses this for," pondered Leo, leaning down and staring closely at the boy's face.

The answer to Leo's pondering could be found in the back room of the gas station where a tool box held ten years worth of rejection letters from every unorganized local and state militia that had a mailing address. Each militia identified itself as a garden- variety political nonprofit organization. The letters were unanimous in stating that the kid just didn't have the brains, balls, or general common sense required to be a successful American outlaw. The kid's point of view was that the members of his future brotherhood were simply testing him to see how much abandonment he could take before cracking. He had specifically chosen to work at this remote gas station to prove that he could go for weeks at a time without any human contact. Far from the main highway where travelers stopped at the shiny, major chain gas stations, this kid rarely had any contact with other human beings. Although he was convinced that people were never far off, believing that many of the militias had spies planted in the desert, watching to see how he was faring in their test.

Just before dozing off that day, the kid was sure he saw movement on the flat, sunlit horizon, perhaps some spies on the move. As he contemplated the best way to respond to this information, the heat of the day had gotten the best of him and he was soon out cold, fast asleep in the hot sun.

Caesar cocked the gun and slammed it into the kid's head.

"Wake up time!"

The kid woke up, took one look at Caesar and Leo, and tried to wriggle away.

Caesar followed him, holding the gun firmly in place. Leo pushed him back into the chair.

"Settle down there. No one's gonna hurt you," he said.

Caesar used the weight of the gun to knock the kid out cold with one swift blow.

"You shouldn't lie, Leo. Come on, help me out," said Caesar.

Leo sighed and helped Caesar drag the kid inside. They deposited him into the back room, gagging and tying him up and then shut the door behind them.

Minutes later, Caesar and Leo came out of the backroom, wearing clean and pressed matching gas station jumpsuits.

"Now it's a fresh start Leo," Caesar said as they made themselves comfortable in the cashier's booth, hidden near the doorway.

"Yeah Caesar. I feel clean," Leo said, running his hands over his new, clean clothes.

Caesar continued inspecting and cleaning the gun, while Leo picked up a newspaper off the counter, following along with his finger as he read. Caesar looked over Leo's shoulder at the paper, and saw mug shots alongside a story detailing a prison break at a different joint.

"How many countries is America invading this week that a perfectly good escape is on page thirteen? What is prison life, a fashion report?" said Caesar.

Leo's eyes never left the newspaper.

"Why are we like this Caesar?" he asked.

"Like what?"

"Like this," Leo said, gesturing at the gun and the door to the backroom where they had just left the gas station attendant.

"Somebody has to be or they would never know the difference. Someone has to enforce good versus evil," Caesar responded.

"Because everyone else does what people tell them, without really thinking through why," Leo said.

"Exactly," said Caesar

"But what we did... All of it... It's OK, right?" Leo asked.

"Of course it's right! Why are you suddenly asking me this now?" demanded Caesar.

"It's just that, we're all clean now... starting out fresh. We haven't really done anything very bad yet. Well, except for beating up that kid back there. But other than that, don't you think... maybe on account of you being a father now and all..."

"Where are you getting this from Leo? What's the matter with you?" Caesar snapped, grabbing the newspaper from Leo and whacking him on the head with it.

Leo swatted Caesar away and moved farther across the cashier's booth.

"Sorry Caesar, but it's just that I've been thinking about what the preachers back in the jail were saying..."

"Don't tell me you're listening to those lazy morons in the world who don't have half the smarts or commitment that we do to follow through with a purpose. You're talking about a society of people who don't know what they're supposed to do or think at any given time, unless—unless they go shopping and look at the decorations," Caesar said with a sudden burst of brilliance.

"I don't get what that has to do with it."

Caesar could tell by the look on Leo's face that he clearly didn't.

"Think about it. A lady goes to the shopping mall and there's all this Christmas stuff up everywhere. "It's the birthday of the Christ child, let us spread the love of the baby Jesus!" Find the same lady halfway through February and it's like Christ who? Jesus who? No idea what you're talkin' about," he explained.

"But what if she's just not religious?" Leo asked

"It's not just religion! Take the fourth of July. Oh I just love America so much! Oh say can you sing! Our forefathers, the *Declaration of Independence*, and all that crap. The next day? These same patriots will look at you like you're crazy. "Declaration of what?" they'll say. They might as well be alien commies, because they'll have no idea what you're talkin' about. Yeah Leo, these are the people you're listening to. Are you gonna let a society like this tell you what's right and what's wrong?" Caesar lectured.

"I guess you're right Caesar. You've never led me wrong yet," Leo said.

"Damn straight, you just gotta trust me. I know what's best for you buddy. I wouldn't lead you wrong. Now we had to break out because I got a new baby and I need to be there for him. If I didn't love you like a brother, I never woulda made you the godfather," Caesar said.

Then he stopped abruptly at the sound of a car engine outside the office window.

"Wait a minute," he said, holding a finger over his lips and gesturing for Leo to stay down.

He peeked over the windowsill and saw a station wagon with a family slowing on the dirt road outside. The dad eyed the broken down, apparently deserted station, shook his head and then continued on down the road.

"Damn. That was a solid set of wheels too," Caesar said.

"Caesar, how are we going to..." Leo said.

"Shhh," Caesar said again.

Caesar realized they couldn't sit here crouched by a busted-out window forever. They were on a reunion mission. He picked up the .45 and aimed it at the door to the backroom.

"Don't worry. We can always bring our hostage with us—and his wheels too," he said.

"What wheels?" asked Leo.

Caesar lined up the gun sight with an imaginary viewing hole through the door leading out back. He saw the young attendant, gagged with a white cloth and chained to a water pipe. Caesar's imaginary sight line extended past the boy to a small window now. It went through the window and outside in the dirt, where a shiny new rust-colored Camaro awaited them out back. It was the real life version of the Hot Wheels car. The desert sun reflecting off the hood created a spotlight that extended up into the heavens.

Still aiming the gun at the door Caesar jumped up and headed out back.

"Leo, the Lord has blessed us yet again! My car has found me!"

Their hostage was starting to come to, looking around wide-eyed at his circumstances and trying desperately to speak through the cloth gag. Leo started to unchain the kid. Caesar glanced out the window at a rusted old, dented Camaro with a cracked back window and a bullet hole in the passenger side door, parked behind the gas station. The car of his dreams had been through a few nightmares.

"We're leaving the kid. " he said.

Leo retightened the chains and Caesar interrupted him, shoving the gun into his hand.

"But he didn't do anything…" Leo said, trying to hand the gun back to Caesar.

"He was sleeping at work, Leo. Now what if he has a son? What kind of example do you think that sets? And if he's not afraid to set a bad example for one thing, what makes you think it won't lead to a ton of other things? He might even be beating his baby's mama," Caesar said.

"Caesar no! That's an awful thing to do," Leo said in horror.

"Anything's possible," Caesar said solemnly, handing the gun back to him.

Leo walked over, looked at the kid for a moment, and then removed the gag from his mouth.

"Any last words?"

"Please sirs," the kid sputtered, "I know why you're here. And I promise you I'm up to the task sirs. I've been preparing and I'm ready to serve."

"What's he talking about Caesar?" Leo asked, turning away from the gun.

"I don't know—sir," Caesar told him sarcastically and then to the kid, "Were those your actual last words or do you actually have something to say?"

"Yes sir. Please go look in that toolbox in the corner… yes that's the one. I've saved all the letters. The return addresses were different but I knew it was all a test. I knew it was one fine group of patriots just like yourselves," the kid said, looking proud of himself.

Caesar flipped through the letters, smiling.

"What is it? What do they say?" Leo asked impatiently, aiming the gun at their hostage.

"Hmmm, well the general theme is pretty patriotic Leo. Our young friend is apparently desperate to make a stand against the national powers that be. He feels that our great nation has lost its way and wants to do his part to help us find it again. He wants to follow in the footsteps of America's very forefathers and declare his independence!" Caesar preached.

"Caesar you keep forgetting I haven't read like you have. What're you talking about?" Leo said, frustrated.

He dried his sweaty palms on the jumpsuit one at a time and transferred the gun from one hand to the other.

"Sorry buddy. Simply put, this young fella right here is a bona fide American patriot, looking for the right opportunity to serve," Caesar told Leo.

He patted the chained up kid on the back. "Isn't that right buddy? We've become a country full of trash and you're looking for an opening as a garbage man."

"Exactly! Yes sir!" the kid exclaimed, beaming.

"Which is really just a small change in uniform," Caesar continued, patting the jumpsuit he'd donned, and the kid nodded.

"Caesar what's the plan here?" Leo said anxiously, wiping his palms again on the jumpsuit.

Caesar stood scratching his chin and thinking.

"Well?" Leo persisted.

"Let's take him with us. Yup, that's what we're gonna do buddy. We're going to bring this future American hero with us on our mission," Caesar announced.

He pushed down a twinge of guilt for using the word "hero," reaching up and touching his dad's dog tags around his neck.

"Anyway," he said, "our twosome just became a threesome. Chains off and off we go."

He looked at Leo, who was still aiming the gun in his shaking hand.

"Here buddy, two hands," Caesar said, guiding Leo's free hand up to the gun and wrapping it around with the tenderness of a father holding the back of his kid's bicycle, teaching him to ride. Leo smiled at him gratefully.

Then, Caesar undid the chains and helped the kid up, shaking his hand.

"Thank you sir—sirs—let me gather up some more supplies for our trip—er mission," he said, rushing out to the front of the store.

Caesar and Leo looked at each other, Leo still aiming the gun at the now unoccupied pipe.

The kid was making a racket out front.

"I'm eager to hear more about the mission sirs!" he yelled out maniacally.

"OK kid, we'll tell you all about it, just hurry it on up," Leo called back.

Caesar nodded at him approvingly and Leo smiled.

The kid finally reappeared in the doorway with about a half a dozen stuffed shopping bags.

"I think we're going to have to leave all that behind son," Caesar said laughing and added, "but I do give you credit for resourcefulness."

The kid dropped the bags on the floor.

"Yes sir," he said.

"C'mon boys let's go," Caesar said.

He hustled Leo and the kid out the back door. Feeling relaxed about their new unofficial partner, Leo loosened his grip on the gun and let it fall to his side. In his excitement, the kid brushed by Leo, pushing him aside as he walked out the door.

"Good thing that didn't happen back in the joint, right buddy?" Caesar joked to Leo. "A new fish might find himself on the receiving end of a lights out beating for that kind of disrespect."

"Yeah, we just might have to teach him a lesson!" Leo joked back, grinning.

The kid turned and looked back and forth between Caesar and Leo with one eyebrow up, the happy-go-lucky demeanor wiped from his face.

"What're you guys talking about?" he asked.

"Oh don't worry, Caesar was just joking you see..." Leo started, still smiling but holding his free hand up in protest.

"I don't get the joke," the kid said, walking back toward them. "Who are you guys anyway?"

"Exactly who you said, my friend, here to reward you for your loyalty and invite you to join us on our mission," Caesar told him, walking over and attempting to put his hand on the kid's shoulder, but the kid jerked it off.

Years of paranoia had taken their toll on the young guy. He was shaking, his eyes darting around, breathing hard. It was Leo's turn to take a shot.

"C'mon buddy there's nothing to be afraid of," Leo said in a fatherly way, the same way Caesar had talked to him time and time again.

He walked over and started to put his free hand on the kid's other shoulder.

"Leo don't!" Caesar cried out, but it was too late.

Seizing his opportunity, the paranoid kid reached out and swiped the .45 out of Leo's hand. He took a step back and with shaking arm, waved the gun maniacally in the air between Caesar and Leo.

As 11-year-old Caesar tried to sneak quietly through the front door, his father tore around the corner from the hallway in his undershorts, brandishing his gun and screaming drunken obscenities at his son.

The memory liquefied in Caesar's brain and drizzled down his throat as sour acid. Then he looked at the teenager in front of him and realized that the kid was terrified, not out to terrorize.

His hands raised, Leo looked with wide eyes to Caesar.

"Tell me son," Caesar asked the kid, "why is it that you want to join a militia to fight against our country instead of join the military to fight for it?"

A shadow from outside the window crossed over the kid's face and all Caesar heard were gasping breaths.

"My dad owned this gas station. And he... he..." the kid was fighting back tears.

"He was in the military?" Leo gently prodded.

"Are you kidding me? He didn't have the balls," the kid laughed, blowing his nose on the sleeve of his jumpsuit.

"Then what is it? What're you really looking for? And how is shooting the two of us going to help you find it?" Caesar asked, glancing at the position of the sun in the sky and mentally counting the minutes being wasted in this dirt lot therapy session.

The kid shook his head and his arms dropped to his sides like lead weights. Leo started to charge forward for the gun but Caesar held him back.

"Whoa buddy, let's hear him out."

The kid nodded at Caesar in appreciation and copped a squat. Caesar motioned to Leo and they both took seats on the ground next to him. The kid seemed to forget that he was still holding the gun, waving it with his hand motions as he told his story. Caesar and Leo periodically ducked to avoid accidentally ending up in the line of fire.

"My dad played by all the rules. He did everything right. He was an honest man and a good husband and father. He loved my mom and me more than anything in the world. He never even took a pack of gum from a convenience store. He..."

"He was a fucking saint OK, we got it! WHAT is the problem then?" Caesar exploded in irritation.

"Yeah, because some of us didn't get to be raised by saints so maybe you should get on to what's wrong with your life instead of what's right with it," Leo chimed in.

The kid looked at them like they were the crazy ones.

"You think he was a saint? Listen guys, I've met a ton of different people in this job and I can tell you there are two types of people that don't exist—saints and demons. Everyone's stuck somewhere in between," the kid said, and stopped to take a breath.

"But if you could—pick one to be—which would you be?" Leo interrupted.

"A demon. Definitely. Saints are weak. That's what did my father in—weakness. He couldn't defend his own family and our way of life so the government took it all away. So I've decided to head in the opposite direction. Everything good can go to Hell as far as I'm concerned. Good is weak," the kid said, looking Leo directly in the eye.

Leo shook his head in disgust.

"Well that does it," Caesar said cheerfully, popping up to his feet and brushing the dirt off his hands and legs.

The other two guys looked up at him in confusion, shielding their eyes against the midday sun.

As they did, in one rapid motion, Caesar reached back down and swiped the gun out of the kid's hand.

"Hey!" the kid protested and tried to get up.

Caesar kicked him in the chest hard, sending him hurtling flat onto the ground, his head hitting the doorstop. The kid lay gasping for breath.

"Now I know I'm no saint and neither is Leo here, we're both sinners just like anyone else. But I would also never aim to be a demon. That's the kind of shit we're both working to get away from and sorry my friend, there's no room for a wannabe demon on this mission. If anything at all, we're on the hunt for a saint," Caesar said.

"Or maybe an angel," Leo added.

Silence from the doorstep.

"C'mon Leo let's getta outta here," Caesar said, rivers of sweat now crawling down his skin under the jumpsuit.

"What do we do about him? What if he talks?" Leo said.

"Well we can't have that kind of liability to the mission can we buddy? Looks like we'd better have an exorcism."

The kid figured out what was going to happen immediately and scrambled to his feet, but it was too late. Caesar and Leo descended on him like desert foxes and dragged him, struggling and screaming for help, back into the gas station, slamming the door behind them. Less than a minute later, a gunshot shook the doorframe of the building, releasing a cloud of desert dust into the thick hot afternoon air.

Ten minutes later, around the other side of the building over at the pumps, Leo kicked the wheels of the beat-up Camaro as Caesar fueled the vintage car.

"What about thou shalt not kill?" Leo asked.

"He thought trying to be a good person makes you weak," Caesar responded. "I can't have my kid growing up around that. Everyone should at least try to be good. That's what makes you strong—the attempt."

Leo nodded.

"OK here goes," Caesar said, starting the car.

"Let 'er rip!" Leo said gleefully.

Caesar started the Camaro's ignition and the car roared to life.

"That's my girl," Caesar said, patting the dashboard.

It backfired loudly, making Leo jump. He was still standing outside the car staring into space.

"Leo!"

"Hey!"

Leo kicked the wheel again in frustration.

"Where are you buddy?" Caesar called through the open passenger side window.

Leo's eyes were glazed over; he was far away.

"At the dinner table again?" Caesar asked.

"Yeah," Leo said, finally climbing into the car and asking, "Will it ever go away?"

"I don't know buddy. All I can say is that once you become a part of a family that looks out for each other a little bit more and has proper moral values, hopefully that table will drift further and further away," Caesar said.

Leo finally got in the car.

"And maybe getting rid of the other demons will help too?" Leo asked hopefully.

"That always helps. Make the world ready for wannabe saints like us," Caesar said as they sped off down the dirt road.

Later the next night, somewhere in southern Nevada, north of Vegas, Caesar and Leo spotted one of their favorite places to spend the night—a church. According to Caesar's best calculations, they were right on track to arrive at Loretta's last known address in just a few days.

Caesar and Leo sat in a pew up in the church's balcony, over-looking the darkened chapel below.

Moonlight streamed in through the stained glass windows and skylights overhead as Caesar counted the money from the day's activities. Leo got up and returned with an empty collection plate, studying his reflection in its shiny flat bottom, surprised at the scruffy grown-up man staring up at him. He was starting to look more and more like his father.

"Good idea," Caesar said.

He grabbed the collection plate and tossed money into it as he counted.

"The preacher always said something about givin' up a piece of what you earn. How much are we gonna leave?" Leo said.

Caesar reached into his pocket and pulled out a tube of lipstick that he had grabbed along with some lady's wallet, and dropped it in the plate. Leo angrily took it out and tossed it on the floor.

"Watch it buddy," Caesar warned him.

"Since when do we steal things we don't need?" asked Leo.

"Since when do you get to ask so many questions?" asked Caesar.

"I just want to be clear on the difference between us and the bad people," said Leo.

"We do what we need to do to get to my son. We can repent later," said Caesar.

"Wouldn't it be better, you know in the Lord's eyes, if we could get where we're going without hurting people so much?" Leo asked.

"You mean hurting women so much. You don't get so upset when it's a man do you? You're perfectly OK with robbing and hurt-ing men aren't you?" Caesar said.

"I just don't see what it all has to do with..." Leo objected.

"It's not your call! A waste is a waste," Caesar exclaimed.

He ripped the collection plate out of Leo's hand and tossed it over the balcony where it landed with a loud clatter of tin and coins on the chapel floor.

"I'm done with your crap, Leo. If you and me—we aren't working together then we won't get there and we won't get to him in time. That's not what God wants Leo. Is that what you want? Is it?" Caesar said.

"Aww, don't say that Caesar... I just thought..."

"I knew something was wrong. You forgot Caesar's commandment number nine—I get to do all the thinking and you get to do what I tell you," said Caesar.

"You sound like *him*!" Leo protested.

He stormed downstairs into the chapel and up the center aisle as Caesar leaned over the balcony tracking him. Leo darted into one of the empty confessionals and slammed the door shut.

Moments later, the curtain divider rippled as Caesar entered the priest's side of the confessional and sat on the wooden bench.

"Dear Lord, please bless my soul and Caesar's soul and all the other souls that we have hurt along the way," Leo said from the kneeler.

"God bless us both buddy... That we survived the no good assholes who gave birth to us," Caesar whispered respectfully.

Leo ignored him.

"Dear Lord, please help us be BETTER than the no good... you know... Let us remember that if we don't change anything, our kids will be better off without us," he prayed.

Caesar came over to Leo's side of the confessional, yanked him out bodily and shoved him into a pew.

"Did it ever occur to you that your father was trying to make you into a man? That's more than I can say for the useless pair of walking ovaries who..." Caesar started.

But Leo was already on his feet, bolting down the aisle toward the altar. Caesar was on his heels. Leo reached the cross and there was nowhere else to go so he spun around.

"Lousy fathers are worse than lousy mothers!" Leo bellowed.

He paused for a reaction but Caesar gave him nothing, taking a certain pleasure in Leo's rage. He carefully masked the satisfied smirk that threatened to reveal the pride he was feeling for Leo for sticking up for himself.

"What do you have against women?" Leo yelled.

Now it was Caesar who turned away, but Leo grabbed his arm. Caesar instinctively elbowed Leo in the gut.

"Murderers trump whores, huh buddy?"

"I want an answer Caesar," Leo demanded, folding his arms sternly.

All signs of a smirk had faded from Caesar's face, replaced with nothing but bitter rage. He knew that Leo deserved more than the partial answers he had given in the past to this question. But right now, all the emotions associated with his childhood memories were raging too powerfully to cut a hole through with words.

"Goodnight Leo," Caesar said, reaching unconsciously around his neck and gripping his father's dog tags.

He pushed by Leo and stormed back up the stairs to the balcony. Leo curled up in a ball on the altar under the cross and stared up at it, imagining Jesus nailed to it, staring down at him lovingly.

The next morning, as the two men climbed back into the Camaro, Caesar ignored Leo's silent glare. But by time they made it to the highway, the silence reminded Caesar of the sickening emptiness of solitary confinement. He decided to throw his loyal buddy a bone.

"The women allow the men to be bad. They're too weak to stop them. Some of them even *make* them bad through their weakness. So nobody's left to protect the kids," he said and then turned the radio on loudly.

Even over the sounds of AC/DC's *Highway to Hell*, Caesar could've sworn he heard Leo's emotional "thank you" float across the front seat to him. He figured that bought him another six months of moderate verbal abuse and bullying, and refusing to answer more painful questions.

"Yeah right," Caesar muttered under his breath, later that morning.

Maybe this was the punishment he had coming to him for humoring Leo's first set of questions. Either way, round two of Leo's deep ponderings came at a church mission where they'd stopped for supplies.

The old nun looked wary, to say the least, when the old car carrying the two smudged and dusty men in gas station jumpsuits pulled up in front of her sacred shelter for the poor, down and out, weary, and in Caesar and Leo's case, opportunist. However, when the strangers got out of the Camaro they flashed boyish smiles so friendly and innocent that the seventy-two year old sister of mercy couldn't help smiling back and motioning the two men inside.

Caesar and Leo spoke to each other through their wide, toothy grins as they entered the mission.

"It's OK to take charity from a woman?" hissed Leo.

Again with the questions.

"It is if she's a woman of God," he hissed back.

"I thought God made all women and men," said Leo through his teeth.

"Yes, but only a few of them admit it," said Caesar as they walked up to the traditionally robed sister.

Caesar looked her right in her pruned, holy eyes and introduced her to his "retarded" little brother, explaining how he was transporting him cross-country to his new home. The movie that inspired this particular brainstorm was one of Caesar's favorite selections for weekly movie night at the prison. There was something about the brotherly love between a hotshot egomaniac and his trusting, but uncannily acute buddy that made Caesar quickly decide that *Rain Man* was the only movie that made sense to emulate.

Instantly charmed, the nun forked over two sleeping bags, bottled water, and one overwhelming sense of validation from a true servant of God.

They tossed the blessed haul into the back seat and made their way through Sin City. Highway after highway, the car stayed on course, courtesy of Leo the human compass.

That night, just over the Arizona border, long after the sun had set, under the vast domed starry sky wrapping around the desert like a velvet quilt, Caesar and Leo laid out their sleeping bags in the dirt and settled in for the night. Before they settled in, they stood and did a 360 sweep of the desert, listening intently even though the last sirens they'd heard were in the distance days ago.

Caesar rolled his head from side to side, admiring the un-caged brilliance of the sky he missed for so long. Each star represented infinity, a chance in every new moment to make better choices.

The blissful, disoriented fog of sleep had nearly overtaken him when he heard the crunch of footsteps in the dirt above his head. The .45 from the kid at the gas station was just out of reach from his fingertips under the blanket.

If the footsteps belonged to a cop and he moved his hand under the covers even slightly, he'd be dead. Of course, he reasoned, one cop would have been a swarm and they'd have already shouted their arrival like a circus coming to town. If the footsteps belonged to someone he'd insulted behind bars, he would have felt fingers around his neck and smelt the fear sweat first. He knew his best chance was if it was a bounty hunter standing over him. They'd bring him in alive just for the money. Caesar kept his hands exactly where they were and his eyes shut.

"I know we both have something the other wants," he said, slowly opening his eyes.

Leo peered down at him quizzically; his rolled up sleeping bag shoved under his arm.

"Commandment number six," Caesar said grabbing, his gun and standing up.

"I didn't mean to sneak up on you Caesar. I was saying good-bye in my head," said Leo.

"Yeah? Where is it you think you're going?" asked Caesar.

"Don't worry Caesar, I didn't take anything," said Leo.

"You know me too well, buddy."

"Yeah I do," said Leo, "That's why I can't do this anymore. I can't go any further than I've already gone."

"Go back to bed Leo. I'll tell you why you're not making any sense in the morning," said Caesar.

Satisfied that his usual nugget of tough love had ended the conversation, he climbed back into his sleeping bag with his gun.

"I can't follow rules that I don't get anymore. That's what got me here in the first place," Leo said.

Caesar sat up, his back to Leo and placed his gun in his lap, loading and reloading the clip over and over, following the bullets with his eyes, catlike in the dark.

"Tell me Leo," he said loading and reloading faster and faster, "after ten years off and on of following, even enforcing my rules, which ones are you suddenly having trouble understanding?"

"The hurting," said Leo. "I don't understand why we need to keep hurting people without being sure about their sins."

"Does anyone for sure know if a man's guilty or not?" asked Caesar.

"My mom did. She knew for sure," said Leo.

Caesar put his gun back together and aimed it out into the desert.

"And when she put that hole in dear old dad," Caesar started.

BANG! He fired a shot into the darkness, slicing through the desert silence and raising a mini dust cyclone where it impacted. He heard Leo yelp in surprise. Caesar nodded in satisfaction and lowered the gun.

"Did that bring your new baby sister back to life?" asked Caesar.

"No," Leo said softly as Caesar dug deeper into the wound.

Caesar read Leo's mind and faced him.

"You could've slipped away from here tonight without me hearing a thing Leo. You've done it before."

"Maybe," said Leo, and he sat on his bag of stuff hanging his head.

"So what is it you want then?"

Leo shrugged.

"I'm not playing this game a second longer buddy," said Caesar. "You tell me what the problem is or get back to bed and never say a word about it again. Those are your choices."

"Killing *him* didn't make the baby alive, just like you said. So what's the point of…" started Leo.

"Your mother, in the only intelligent thing she ever did except for giving birth to you, made it so he could never kill another baby," said Caesar.

"Promise me for your baby, my godchild," said Leo, "that from now on we'll only hurt…. Or kill… people who we know for sure…"

"Oh for God's sake Leo, I don't know anything for sure," Caesar snapped. "Except that if I stop trusting my instincts now, after all this time, it will be nothing but trouble for you, me, Loretta and my kid. I can't take that chance Leo. I have a responsibility to all of us."

Leo stared into Caesar's eyes, with his eerie uncomfortable gaze.

"You think of me like family Caesar?" he asked in surprise.

Caesar met his gaze head on.

"Buddy if it was me sitting across that dining room table I would have killed that son of a bitch long before your mom had a chance."

CHAPTER SIX
BANKRUPT

A goddamn bank robbery! Caesar couldn't believe Leo had finally talked him into it. The bank practically called out to him onto the dusty, sweltering highway. It was actually Leo's voice and it was more nagging than calling.

Leo's bank robbery campaign had started before they left prison and his persuading was constant and relentless. He chose not to hear Caesar every time he reminded Leo that they were not bank robbers.

He remembered when they were back in their cell the night before the breakout, just after lights out, when Leo had said this:

"But why not? It's harmless compared to holding up all those little stores with guns and maybe hurting someone. Besides the bank has plenty of money to put back in the drawers after we leave anyway," Leo persisted.

In the bottom bunk, Caesar looked up and wondered if Leo had learned anything at all from him. Then he smiled, savoring the preview of being a frustrated dad.

"Because banks don't care about which kind of people they're watching money and valuables for. If we broke in and took money, how do we know whether it's from decent people or bad seeds? I'd hate to accidentally rip off a good man," Caesar said patiently.

"Seems easier than getting a little bit of money at a time like you want to," Leo said from overhead.

"We get a little at a time because that's all we need and we know who we're getting it from so we can pay 'em back," Caesar replied.

"Still waiting for the day that happens," Leo mumbled.

"What was that buddy?"

The guard came by and the matter was temporarily settled. Caesar thought it was put to bed permanently until Leo kept scratching at it once they were out on the road.

Leo's bank robbery campaign had continued back at the gas station right after they got out of prison, once the kid attendant was tied up in the back. Caesar emptied the register, frowning.

"What?" Leo asked, dutifully acknowledging Caesar's distress.

"What do you mean what? Can you count?"

Caesar crammed a measly wad of cash from the register into the pocket of his brand new gas station jumpsuit.

"Well you know how we could've gotten more…"

Leo knew he was pushing it.

"Shut it Leo!"

Caesar stormed into the gas station's backroom to check on the chained up kid.

That wasn't enough to make Leo drop the subject. The next banking reminder would require no words. As the two rode their newly acquired classic car down the highway, they passed a sign advertising a new bank branch in a neighboring town. Caesar felt the heat of Leo's stare on the right side of his face. He ignored him and blasted the radio. The bank conversation had begun to bore Caesar and he was hoping Leo would also get bored with the old-fashioned notion.

But much to his surprise and Leo's, when they were in the church balcony later that night Caesar found himself resurrecting the bank robbery conversation again. They sat in the church balcony looking down at the empty, dark chapel.

"This place loses something without the preacher speaking the Lord's words and all the people following along with the procedures. Barely seems like a church at all," Caesar remarked.

"Really?" Leo asked. "I think it's even more of a church with no one in it. I feel like I can get closer to God this way. 'Specially since on Sundays, you've got one group of people that doesn't know why they showed up, and another who showed up for the wrong reasons."

Leo paused and closed his eyes, letting the natural divinity of the space wash over his soul.

"Here's the problem with banks," Caesar exclaimed suddenly, his voice bouncing off the statue of a crucified Christ.

"What?"

Leo rushed back to Caesar's moment as quickly as his mind could carry him.

"You wanted to know why I won't rob a bank and here's your answer."

Caesar delivered his newest gospel to his only rapt follower.

"Banks are a lie. They sucker people into trading their real hard-earned money for a worthless piece of paper. What do you think they really have back in all those vaults that they need such a horse and pony show to protect, with all the doors and keys and heavy steel walls? You think it's actually the people's hard-earned money that men sweat blood for? No!"

"All they've got back there are great grandma's favorite rings, a yellow stock certificate that hasn't been worth anything for a century, great grandpa's ashes and some other piece of useless shit that would be just as safe in a shoebox under a bed. But people have been brainwashed into thinking that you're supposed to put stuff in a bank because IT'S special—because THEY'RE special. Banks are nothing but pomp and circumstance to make people think their money is more special than it really is."

He continued on, pacing quickly up and down the church balcony as he preached.

"How're they going to have room for everyone's money in that one little room anyway? No Leo, all banks keep for the people is a promise, that if they ever need any money it will be there for them. And I don't trust anyone making promises, especially about money. I don't care what kind of fancy lobby and lighted sign they have out front telling me the weather. What the hell does a bank know about the weather anyway?"

Leo took a minute as usual to absorb Caesar's latest preaching.

"But where do the ladies behind the counter get people's money to give them?" Leo finally asked.

Caesar guffawed.

"All part of the dog and pony show buddy. You see they give them just enough to make it seem like they've got enough for everyone. But think of this—what if everyone needed their money at the same time? You'd see those nice ladies behind the counter run for the hills in a hurry because they know there's not enough money to go around."

Leo sifted through the paper money in the collection plate as he mulled this over. As usual, everything that Caesar told him spawned about a hundred new questions, like balloons being released all over his brain.

"Then why do the police go to the trouble of locking up bank robbers if there isn't much to steal?"

Caesar didn't miss a beat.

"Just like not everyone on the outside knows their job well, not everyone who gets locked away is a professional in their work either. Some guys are just starting out, figuring out their way and they get picked up for stupid little shit. Robbing banks is like amateur night. But it can also be like what the TV calls a 'gateway drug' that can lead to bigger things. That's why the law is always on the lookout for guys like that."

Leo automatically recited one of Caesar's commandments.

"If the law is looking for you left, then go right."

"So you finally understand why we don't rob banks," Caesar said patiently.

"Yep," Leo mumbled, counting the money in the collection plate again.

"But just the same, I'd still wanna take a look in one of those backrooms sometimes," Leo said and then added quickly when he saw the look on Caesar's face, "Not because I don't trust you but just because I'm curious. Assuming there's no law there and someone left the doors open. I wouldn't want anyone to get hurt on account of me being a curious cat."

"Yeah I guess if the situation presented itself I'd take a peek too buddy," Caesar chuckled again.

Leo exhaled deeply, relieved that Caesar was no longer mad at him.

As luck would have it, a couple days after they left the church, the situation presented itself. Caesar noticed the bank before Leo, a shiny new structure that looked as if a helicopter had dropped it there the day before without getting a speck of dirt on it during the drop. Leo thought that meant the bank would have a lot more money than any other ones.

They were sitting behind a travel center, crouched behind some dumpsters eating the remains of paying patrons' fast food lunches out of wrinkled greasy paper bags. Leo spotted the structure across the street. It was impossible to miss really—a diamond in a sewage treatment plant.

"There's no cars or people around so we could do it quick," he pointed out, trying to sound casual and focusing on his food.

"Well, we do need the cash," Caesar said, examining the remains of the fast food leftovers.

Leo's restlessness quickly wore off on Caesar and the bank job became a rush job from the start. If it hadn't, and Caesar had been his usual methodical self, he might've noticed some things about this bank in particular. For instance, out front, the lights on the bank sign that always knew the correct time and temperature were out. Leo almost pointed out how the only vehicle in the tiny, newly paved parking lot was a beat up old VW beetle. But one look at Caesar's impatient eyes and fidgety hands made him keep quiet.

Caesar had Leo stroll by the front door once to check for security. For lack of any, the two opted for an old west approach—through the front door and with fanfare. Except instead of chaps, studs and bandanas, Caesar and Leo wore filthy gas station jumpsuits and held napkins over their faces.

"This is a stick up!" Leo shouted jubilantly at the empty lobby.

"What did I tell you about the movie lines?" Caesar scolded him.

"I thought you wanted to be fast so I figured we should get to the point," Leo argued.

"Don't worry this will be fast. It looks like this place opened yesterday. The money truck probably left an hour ago," said Caesar.

"OK but where is everyone?" asked Leo, searching the bank for any signs of life.

"Let's go," Caesar grabbed Leo by the elbow and pushed him behind the counter toward the built-in safe.

Its enormous, thick steel door was swung wide open revealing a shiny metal room with row after row of safe deposit boxes.

"Coming Caesar," he said, shuffling with his head down behind his partner into the safe, and closing it behind him with a resounding thud.

A frail female voice startled them.

"You shouldn't have done that, dear."

The little old lady was standing in the corner of the room, gripping her purse in one hand and a narrow steel box in the other. Dressed in her Sunday best, complete with wrinkled, nylon stockings slipping down her white furry legs, white gloves and a hat, both men mistook her for an apparition, haunting them from their respective Sunday churchgoing pasts. Caesar thought she was his church organist. Leo thought she was his mother.

"We shouldn't have done what?" asked Caesar.

"That door," she gestured with her white glove toward the enormous closed vault door, "only opens from the outside."

Caesar and Leo looked back at the door based. Caesar normally feared no woman, except ones that appeared in his life at odd times for odd reasons. He could see on Leo's face that he felt the same way.

"There's no way out now," the old woman continued as she walked toward them.

She finally reached them and Caesar and Leo saw that she wasn't a ghost at all. She was just a little old lady with a purse in one hand and a safe deposit box in the other, standing there smiling sweetly at them, without so much as a glance at the gun that Caesar held at his side.

"Should we shoot her?" Leo asked, sounding a bit off balance at the surprise of the situation.

"No you idiot, we shouldn't shoot her!" Caesar mimicked condescendingly.

The old woman continued to smile sweetly at them both. Caesar wasn't sure if she was senile or up to something. He tightened his grip on the gun and looked at her suspiciously.

"Well why not?" Leo asked impatiently.

"First of all, how is that going to get us out of here? And secondly, the way these vaults are, the bullet would ricochet and kill us all," Caesar said, motioning at row after row of steel safe deposit boxes lining the walls around them.

"Hey," Leo asked the woman, "what're you doing?"

Caesar pointed the gun at her.

The old woman was rifling through the narrow rectangular steel safe deposit box.

"You might as well put the gun down son, before you accidentally kill us all," she said, glancing up at him. "Like you said."

Then she returned to sifting through the pile of papers in the box, occasionally making contact with heavier objects that clanked against the side of the box, the sounds reverberating around the tin room.

"Caesar I'm starting to get worried about how we're gonna get outta here," Leo said anxiously, banging the vault door in places and kicking the bottom of it.

Caesar strode over to join him, with his best air of authority. Then, he checked all the places around the door that Leo had already checked.

"Ah," the woman said cheerfully, "I found it."

Both men jumped back, when she pulled an old but still very sharp military knife from the safe deposit box. She admired it, looking it over and caressing it lovingly.

"Oh shit Caesar, we're done for," Leo murmured under his breath.

"Leo don't be an idiot. You think granny is gonna suddenly go psycho on us? Why would she do that?" Caesar said just as quietly.

"Why do we do what we do? Who the hell knows what kind of commandments SHE'S operating from?" Leo asked, pressing his back into the vault door to put as much space between he and the woman as possible.

"Well even if she did buddy, I'd use the gun on her at close range and do my best to rule out any ricochets," Caesar reassured him.

The old woman placed the box on the floor so she could give the knife her full attention.

"Do you know," she said, "how I got this?"

"No ma'am," Leo said.

Caesar looked at him and raised his eyebrow. *Ma'am?*

Leo shrugged.

"Figured it couldn't hurt to show some respect to a lady who is also our elder, especially seeing as how our elder's got a knife."

"My husband Arthur had an older brother named Jim. Arthur was only about ten years old when Jim got drafted and headed over to fight in World War One."

"Is that a fact?" Caesar asked.

"Yes it is young man," the granny said, looking at Caesar with narrow knowing eyes.

He instantly lowered his eyes to the floor in shame, although for what reason, he couldn't say.

"A couple years later, when Arthur was just becoming a teenager, Jim came back from the war. He walked in the front door of the house, still in his Army uniform with dried up bloodstains that even good old-fashioned military elbow grease couldn't remove. The whole family gathered around but Arthur's mother wouldn't let Jim walk in past the foyer before stripping off his dirty clothes."

She paused for a moment, giving Caesar and Leo the up and down once over of their own filthy clothes. Leo flushed red in embarrassment.

"But before Jim would take off his uniform, he insisted on having a chat with Arthur so the two boys went outside and sat on the sidewalk curb. As soon as they sat down, Jim reached in his pocket and pulled out this knife and handed it to his younger brother and told him, 'I've done everything I can with this. It's yours now.'"

"Wow," Leo murmured, totally engrossed in the story.

"Do either of you boys have older brothers?" the old woman asked Caesar and Leo.

"No ma'am," Leo answered quickly.

"My parents could barely manage me," Caesar said with a smile, but stopped when the woman did not return the smile.

"My father was a veteran of the Vietnam War by the way, ma'am," he added.

This time it was Leo who looked at him with one raised eyebrow.

"That's all well and good son but what have *you* done?" she asked Caesar.

Leo took a step back and waited for the coming explosion. But it never came. Normally this would be a call to arms, but all Caesar did this time was reach around his neck and grab his father's dog tags, never taking his eyes off the old woman. He saw himself standing outside his house looking in the bedroom window at the dead bodies of his parents. He remembered wanting to rush back inside and join them, curling up in the fetal position between them. The pain was unbearable.

"What did your husband do with the knife after that?" Caesar asked her.

She looked down at the worn dagger.

"Not much of anything really. What's a young boy supposed to do with a grown man's knife, a knife that took the lives of other grown men in a whole other country so far away he could barely wrap his mind around it? No, Arthur put the knife away in a cigar box in the back of his closet. At first because he was afraid of it—overwhelmed at the thought of what it had done. Then, later on, when he found out his bad lungs would keep him out of the next world war; Arthur became ashamed by the knife. He knew his brother had been braver then he'd ever have the chance to be."

She paused again in the heavy silence of the vault. Caesar and Leo were statues, staring not just at her, but also at the ghosts of the conflicted men she'd carried with her into the bank that day.

"I never even knew about the knife myself," she said, "until just last month when the lawyer read my husband's will which included a handwritten letter, telling the whole story. Arthur ended the letter with how ashamed he was never to have become half the man his brother was. In his own eyes anyway. I happen to have a somewhat different opinion."

She smiled and turned away for a moment.

Leo turned away too, raising his elbow to dab his eyes.

"He left the keys to this exact safe deposit box with his lawyer. And it has taken me all these weeks to get up the courage to come down here and see the knife for myself. To lay eyes on my beloved husband's secret shame."

She ran her dry pruned hands up and down the knife, as if searching for even more clues.

"What are you going to do with it now?" Caesar asked her, still grasping the dog tags around his neck.

She held the knife out toward Caesar, handle first.

"Why?" he asked, not moving to take it from her.

"We both know this knife needs to be redeemed. And I get the feeling you're the one to redeem it," she said.

"How am I supposed to do that?" he asked, taking a step forward, looking at the knife.

"You'll know," she said.

Caesar took the knife in his hand and let the cold steel of the blade settle into his palm. He wondered about the men on its receiving end. How old were they? Which countries were they from? What were their last words? Did they fight back?

"I'll do my best ma'am," he said.

The old woman nodded, and returned the tin box into its place in the wall and stood next to it clutching her purse, staring at the door of the vault.

"Leo I wonder which one has killed more people, the gas station gun or Jim's knife?" Caesar said, still examining the knife.

"Does it matter?" Leo asked.

"What do you mean does it matter? Of course it matters. Every weapon is born with its own purpose. My dad's gun was meant to kill my whore of a mom… sorry ma'am. And your dad's gun was meant to set you free," Caesar said.

"I don't feel very free right now," Leo said.

"Temporary setback buddy. I'm sure of it," Caesar reassured him.

"Yeah sure, you always are," Leo muttered.

"Really? Are you doing this now? In front of company?"

"Give me a break Caesar I'm tired! I'm tired of all of this and now we're standin' here waiting for the police to come and put us back in jail or maybe worse, and you're acting like it's not a big deal. You're all chattin' away like usual without a care in the world, this poor lady just buried her husband, and she's so scared she hands over the last thing he left for her. What's the matter with you?" Leo yelled loud enough to make the tin boxes rattle in the wall.

He was horrified to realize that in that moment, he wanted to kill Caesar.

"Fine. You take this then. You get to decide the purpose of this gun from now on," Caesar said, thrusting the .45 into Leo's hand.

"Caesar I didn't mean that," Leo protested, fearfully trying to hand it back.

"I don't need it anyway. I got Jim's knife."

"Son it might have started as Jim's knife, but it ended as Arthur's knife. Show some respect," the old woman stated quietly from the corner.

"Now wait just one minute here!" Caesar started, finally losing his temper.

He had the same sensation as back at the gas station, rivers of sweat dripping down his body making him itch unbearably. He knew they needed to get out of there or he'd lose it and make a mistake.

His panicked thoughts were interrupted by the sudden emergence of two construction workers with bright yellow hardhats climbing out of the floor in the middle of the room. The workers were halfway out of the hole, standing on the top rungs of their respective ladders, before they noticed what they'd walked into. They froze in place, blinking around at Caesar, Leo, and the old woman.

"What the…." said Leo in confusion.

"How can a steel vault have a regular floor?" Caesar demanded raising the knife, his eyes bulging wildly, his breath coming quick.

Leo looked at him nervously.

"What are you people doing in here? This bank's not set to open for another week. We're here to put the steel bottom in," one of the workers said.

"My son is the regional vice president of this bank chain," the old woman said, "He let me in to retrieve something from my husband's safe deposit box that the lawyer transferred here."

She saw that not a single person in the room believed her.

"Well actually gentlemen my son is the only person who technically knows I'm here and the only reason he let me is because these items are what you would call sentimentally valuable, but nothing worth breaking into a bank for."

The workers then turned toward Caesar and Leo, and spotting the knife and the gun, raised their hands in the air.

"We're not looking for any trouble guys. Let's say we showed up here to do our jobs and there was some problem with the foundation and we couldn't get in," one of them said.

Caesar took a step toward the hole, raising the knife.

"Caesar no!" Leo cried out.

But it was the old woman who got his attention.

"Is that all you've learned today young man? What would your father say?" she asked Caesar.

All he could do was utter was an animalistic war cry as he lunged for the center of the room, wrapping his arm around a worker's neck like a boa constrictor, hugging the knife blade tightly against the skin. The other worker froze in place, soaking the crotch of his work trousers.

"Caesar WHAT are you doing?" Leo asked angrily.

"I can't take it anymore buddy. You've been right all along. This isn't right but I don't know how to make it right either. We're in too deep you know? I just wanna go home. I wanna crawl out of here and go home," Caesar said.

Then he realized his face was wet. Against all realistic odds, he was crying. This had to be what the end of a long story felt like.

Leo was speechless. He looked at the gun in his hand and Caesar noticed.

"Buddy if you want to do the right thing and shoot me to save this innocent life, I wouldn't blame you. I wouldn't even hold it against you, in the afterlife and all. I just wanna go home," he told Leo.

"What's at home?" the old woman asked quietly from the corner.

Caesar hung his head and choked back a sob.

"My dad…. He's waiting for me. I gotta tell him how I failed. I tried my best to do better, to find a good woman, to have a family, to be a good man and a father but I couldn't do it. I couldn't make it all the way," he said through tears, his knife wielding arm shaking against the worker's neck.

"But Caesar you haven't failed yet. We only have a little ways to go," Leo told him.

Caesar shook his head, unable to speak.

"Caesar, HE'S waiting for you. Not in the afterlife. But here, with Loretta," Leo said, going over and putting a comforting hand on Caesar's back.

"Leave me here. You can do a better job as godfather than I can as a father. You're a better man than me Leo and you know it."

"I won't go without you Caesar. You're the only family I have," Leo insisted.

"There's nothing waiting for you at home son," the woman told Caesar. "The memories that you see in your mind were erased a long time ago. You didn't notice the moment it happened because you'd already moved on with your life. But they're all gone. There's nothing left to go back to. All you can do now is create new ones."

Caesar exhaled with a groan and without a word, took the knife back, slid it in his pocket, and then slid into the hole in the floor, disappearing. Leo and the old lady looked at each other.

The old woman nodded to him.

"Go on. I'll explain everything to these brave young men here," she said, nodding toward the terrified workers.

"Thank you ma'am," Leo called out as scurried down the ladder, disappearing into the floor.

Farther down the tunnel, as he crawled through the dirt tunnel under the bank toward the light, Caesar felt his head swimming in confusion.

"What the hell just happened?" he murmured as they finally reached the mouth of the tunnel and the freshly painted orange metal grate the workers had unlocked on their way in.

He stood up, tilting his face up into the sunlight and closing his eyes.

"Caesar," Leo said uncertainly, walking up behind his friend.

"It's OK buddy. Moment of temporary insanity. I'm fine now," Caesar reassured him.

Leo nodded.

Maybe it was the exhaustion and stress of being on the run. Or maybe there wasn't enough oxygen pumped into that little room. But Caesar was sure the whole thing had been a dream. After all, he didn't rob banks. And in real life, he never would have let a babbling wrinkled bag talk down to him like that. His hand tightened around the World War I knife as he and Leo ran across the parking lot back to the Camaro to escape—again.

CHAPTER SEVEN
BLOOD BEAR

Tonya should have known better than to get in the pickup truck. It smelled like fast food grease and its driver wasn't a rose garden either. She decided to name him McSmelly. She tried not to think of how many species of microscopic organisms were reproducing in his scruffy brown overgrown beard. She immediately regretted accepting the ride.

But she'd already been hanging around the truck stop for days trying to hustle a way out of Fresno, where the semi truck near the homeless shelter had discarded her. She was desperate to break free again. She still wasn't sure where she was going, but anywhere was better than here. She would have accepted a ride from the devil himself. McSmelly could've been his brother.

Everything had been going fairly well with him from Fresno across to Mammoth and then down south through Nevada. Tonya had mastered the art of breathing through her nose so the toxic fumes didn't completely overcome her. She endured his frequent sideways glances slithering up and down her body, leaving her skin feeling clammy. She pretended to sleep for most of the way, squeezing her belongings tightly between her legs.

Everything was fine until McSmelly tried to auction Tonya off as a hooker on his CB radio. The most ambitious of Nevada's brothels took to the airwaves, advertising mostly to their target audience—truckers. But anyone with a CB could claim a piece of the action.

"Good afternoon gentlemen, this is Eve over at the Pink Lady," the gravelly voice crackled out of the CB radio.

McSmelly grinned and turned up the volume. Tonya was taken so off guard that she forgot to keep faking sleep and looked at the radio.

"Yeah, I thought that might get your attention sweetheart," he snickered.

"We've got seven lovely ladies all excited to meet you," Eve continued to crackle. "We've also got cold beer and showers."

Eve reeled off directions to the brothel and gave out a phone number, with all the bravado of a 411 operator. Even after growing up around hookers who made regular rounds at the trailer park, Tonya was impressed with Eve's entrepreneurial spirit. If prostitution were legal where she grew up in California, she was quite certain that she would have been waiting for her mom to get off work at a whorehouse instead of a diner. They probably would've had more money that way too.

She suddenly wondered what kind of life that mistress Eve had carved out for herself as a small business owner and was tempted to ask McSmelly to follow the directions to the Pink Lady. Looking over at his leering Cheshire cat grin and growing erection in his pants, she figured it wouldn't take a whole lot of convincing. He saw Tonya watching and as she rolled her eyes and focused her attention on the road, he unhooked the CB mouthpiece.

"How much?" he asked Eve through the radio.

"Sir I can't tell you that over the radio," Eve sighed in a semi-professional tone that suggested she did have a legitimate customer service related job at some point in her life.

McSmelly chuckled and hit the transmit button again, winking at Tonya as if they were sharing a secret. Tonya kept her attention focused on the ribbon of dirt and sagebrush unfurling outside her window.

"Well, can you at least tell me how many Ben Franklins I should bring?" he asked Eve, pressing his stained, cracked lips into the mouthpiece.

"I can't tell you that sir."

"Can you at least promise me a discount?" he persisted.

"I'm sorry sir. If you would just come and see us..." Eve started.

"Well hell, if you're not going to give me any kind of deal I might as well take my chances with whatever amateur piece of trash I pick up on the side of the road," the burly man said, winking at Tonya.

He turned the volume down on the radio. Eve was no longer sufficiently entertaining to him so he turned his attention back to the hot piece of ass currently occupying his passenger seat.

"How about it, Vivian darling? I could drop you off to see Eve and fill out a job application if you want," he chuckled, using the first name that Tonya made up, when he picked her up.

"No thanks," she mumbled.

She kept her gaze glued out the window and hoped McSmelly would once again lose interest if she ignored him. But apparently the images of Eve's lovely ladies had him too riled up. He reached over and started caressing her thigh. Up until now he'd only dared paw at her shoulder, feigning the role of a concerned father figure.

"You sure about that?" he asked as they passed the exit number that Eve had mentioned. "A pretty girl like you with nowhere to go could probably do real well for herself at a place like that."

Tonya finally turned away from the window. McSmelly was smiling until he saw the icy glare that she was presently shooting across the cab.

"Even if I did go to the trouble of filling out an application, Eve probably wouldn't hire me anyway," she said.

"Why's that?" he asked, now keeping his eyes on the road to avoid the ice.

"I wouldn't pass the health exam," she answered seriously.

"If you're trying to convince me you got crabs or the clap or something so I won't pull this truck off into the brush and have my way with you right now, it's no use," McSmelly laughed.

"Why, you have them too? Have you already made friends with Eve's lovely ladies?" Tonya fired back.

McSmelly threw back his head, laughing so hard that he almost steered the truck right off the road. Tonya grabbed hold of the door handle, looking for an opportunity to eject. But they were still going too fast.

"No, I'm saying that I know you're full of shit. I've known that since I picked you up. I haul girls like you all the time," he said.

"Like me?"

"Yeah. Poor little pretty things that get to a certain age and decide the world has done nothing but shit all over them. So they take off from their nice warm home with three squares every day to find out where the road goes, figuring it has to be better than where they started," he said.

"Is that a fact?" Tonya said.

She was bored all over again. For a moment she thought she might have to deal with a messy self-defense situation. Then she realized that this guy was even more full of shit than he thought she was.

"Yeah, it's a fact and let me tell you, Vivian. I've been on the road enough to tell you that the only place it leads is back to where you started. There's no yellow brick road, no Oz and no miracles," he said, trying to pass himself off as some sort monster truck messiah.

"We'll see," was all Tonya said in reply to this load of horseshit.

"Yeah we will."

She looked down at his filthy fingernails digging into her thigh once again and sighed. She knew that she'd have to do something messy to get out of this and would much rather have taken a nap instead.

As McSmelly overconfidently kept his eyes on the road instead of her, Tonya quickly and quietly slid her hand into her rucksack, never more than an arm's length away, and withdrew the folding hunting knife with the serrated edge that her father had given her for self-protection as soon as she turned thirteen and the boys in the trailer park started noticing her. She slid the knife up the sleeve of her hoodie sweatshirt. He wouldn't see the knife until the next time they stopped, at an isolated rest stop.

Tired of playing the coy game, he finally forced her into the backseat of his pickup truck at gunpoint. Lying in the backseat with her pants forced down, she'd convinced him to let her keep her sweat-shirt on to stay warm in the chilly evening air. By that point there was barely any blood left to power his brain so he grunted in agreement. He was already focused on getting his own pants off by then.

As he climbed on top of her, a delirious grin painted grossly across his face, Tonya shook the knife out of her sleeve and cleanly into her hand. Feigning putting her arms over her head in a position of bondage, all while smiling sweetly at him, she unfolded the knife behind his neck. He never heard a thing. He was too busy trying to align himself over Tonya's private parts to ensure a clean entry that wouldn't bend his own part uncomfortably.

"You know, some people don't like to play Russian roulette with their lives. Then some people can play it all day long," she said.

"Huh?" the animal grunted, caught off guard.

Tonya aimed the sharpened tip of the knife directly at the hollow space where the man's neck met his shoulders as he prepared for his grand entrance. She beat him to it, jamming the knife into the side of his neck with a surprising amount of force, twisting the blade as she drove it in. He reared back like a bear that had just been shot, roaring in pain. He grabbed his neck, which was pulsing a red flood all over the back seat; Tonya withdrew the knife, whipped it around and got him in the gut.

As he continued to yell, pant and writhe, she pulled her pants on, grabbed her stuff and was out of the truck in moments, sprinting to the rest stop. Safely in the woman's restroom, cloaked in the company of strangers, she dipped the knife in the toilet and stared at the ribbons of blood swirling in watery circles. Tonya was about to put the knife in her rucksack, when she pictured shooting flames, a giant hairy fist coming at her face, and finally, McSmelly with his head thrown back, blood shooting out of his neck.

"Enough," she said.

She slid the knife into the small tin feminine product trashcan and vowed to only accept rides from women drivers from that point on.

Later, in yet another big rig on a rural interstate somewhere between Hell and wherever the hell it was that Tonya would eventually end up, she was fighting with a middle-aged woman semi truck driver.

Even during this heated pseudo-mother-daughter argument Tonya was now engaged in, she still shuddered, remembering the bloody confrontation from the night before. Even though she'd taken a sink bath at the rest stop, she still smelled McSmelly's body odor and blood. The truck she was in now reeked of tobacco which seemed to contradict the glittery animal stickers and rainbows and pictures of the woman's grandkids decorating the dashboard.

Once she got to talking to her in the rest stop bathroom, Tonya decided the woman was a safe bet. She wasn't experienced at "girl talk" but thought that maybe it would do her some good. Maybe the female driver would be her human atlas based on all her trucking miles, and suggest a good place for Tonya to eventually land. As they pulled away from the rest stop in the giant semi, Tonya felt optimistic for the first time in a very long time.

What she hadn't bet on, however, was this woman turning into her mother before her eyes.

"That's still no reason to just pick up and leave," the woman was saying.

"I didn't leave! I escaped!" Tonya said back.

"If you're the only one who knows the difference then it doesn't matter," the woman said.

"It matters to me. It means I have principles," Tonya said.

"I'm just saying..." the woman started.

"No. You're not," Tonya said fiercely.

She spotted an upcoming exit.

"Drop me here," she demanded.

"Why here?" the woman asked.

"Because I said so!" Tonya answered.

The semi lumbered slowly down the exit ramp and rolled to a stop at the bottom. Tonya tumbled down the platform steps with her guitar and rucksack and looked back up at her temporary mom.

"Where is this by the way?" she called up into the cab.

The woman laughed, rolled her eyes and shook her head.

"Welcome to the Grand Canyon state. Planning on some sightseeing?" she called down.

Tonya laughed, waved her off and started walking toward the combination gas station and convenience store off to the right.

On her way across the parking lot into the store, Tonya stormed by Caesar, who was trying to fill an old car with gas, grumbling in frustration as he struggled with an even older gas pump. Leo was over by the store, standing with his nose pressed against the window, admiring a swivel rack of stuffed animals.

"Caesar are we gonna go inside?" Leo called out.

"Hold on, I'm busy," Caesar snapped.

As Tonya lingered in the parking lot, Leo returned to staring longingly through the window as Caesar started to bang the handle against the gas pump. She walked over and took the pump handle from him. He tried to grab it back and push her out of the way.

"Watch it," she warned.

Caesar started to push her again but stopped when she glanced up at him and he caught the fire coming out of her eyes. He had never seen that kind of life in a woman's eyes before.

Intrigued, he held up his hands in mock surrender, took a step backward and folded his arms, challenging her. Tonya glared at him, took the safety latch off and pumped the gas, never taking her eyes off him. She finished and replaced the handle on the pump.

"Good job," Caesar said.

"Give me a break," she said.

Caesar looked around trying to figure out how this little pixie with the fire in her eyes had arrived.

"Are you lost?" he asked.

"No," she said, brushing by him.

He continued to stare, trying to figure her out.

"Nice car," she called out over her shoulder before entering the store, with a slight swing in her narrow hips.

Caesar joined Leo over at the window and they watched Tonya enter the convenience store and start dropping inexpensive items into a shopping basket as she strolled through the store in absolutely no rush.

At the counter, a tall, skinny thirty something guy with side-burns swept the store with his eyes in a state of hyper alert and his thin lips spread into a forced likeable grin. The guy instantly made Caesar's skin crawl.

"Should we go pay for the gas?" Leo asked.

"I already told you, we'll pay all these places back once I settle down and earn some money. Our situation shouldn't be their problem," Caesar said.

"Can't we go inside for just a minute?" Leo asked.

"What's up buddy?" Caesar asked.

"I wanna go shopping… like the girl," Leo said, pointing to Tonya.

They watched through the window as she calmly made her way to the back of the store with her full shopping basket. At the same time a little boy broke free from his mother and ran over to a turnstile full of stuffed animals over by the window.

The turnstile was surrounded by an assortment of souvenir items like hats, key chains, coffee mugs, and t-shirts. Every last piece of dusty inventory sat waiting for all the tourists who nine out of ten times, blew right past this exit ramp in favor of the next one. That was the exit featuring a full-scale clean and shiny travel center, modern fast food chains, and other tourist friendly amenities.

The boy had his eyes on a stuffed teddy bear wearing a little red teddy bear t-shirt with a drawing of the state of Arizona on it. He removed it from the rack and examined it closely before his mother rushed over to retrieve him. The boy burst into tears as he was forced to leave the teddy bear behind on the floor. Leo stared down at the teddy bear and then back at the girl, curious about what she was planning. She caught Leo's eye, smiled and looked up toward the front of the store. The moment the over eager clerk turned around to get a pack of cigarettes out of the case from behind the counter, she slipped quietly out the back door with her full shopping basket. Caesar smiled.

"Did you see that?" Leo whispered.

"Yeah, I saw it," Caesar responded.

"Well aren't you mad at her for doing that?" Leo asked.

Caesar hated the question and hated himself even more for questioning himself. These new thoughts suddenly floating around his head were more annoying than an anonymous mosquito in a dark bedroom.

"As a matter of fact, my short-sighted buddy, it does not bother me," Caesar said, faking it.

Leo's face was a question mark.

"See that clerk up there? I've been watching him since we got here and I've figured out some stuff about him," Caesar said.

Leo pressed his face up against the window and watched.

"See how he jumped to attention as soon as that lady and her kid came to the counter to check out? I can almost feel his eagerness to please oozing through the glass. Look, I think he's even trying to upsell them some Tic Tacs," Caesar said.

"So what? He just wants to do a good job, nothing wrong with that," Leo said.

"Nope. I know the difference between a good man wanting to do a good job and a bad man—well a once bad man anyway—trying to make amends. This is a man that started out like us Leo. He made some choices in life, got caught for the ones society happened to disagree with, did his time, and got out, just like us," Caesar explained. "That mother fucker did time and this piece of shit job is the only thing he has left."

"Mm hmm," Leo said as the woman and her kid exited the store and walked by them.

"But mooommmmmyyy I wanted the teddddyyyy bear!" the boy squealed.

"Mommy said no!" the woman barked, practically dragging her child back to the car by his arm.

Leo stared at them until Caesar grabbed him by the elbow and walked back to the car.

"But do you want to know where that particular ex-con, standing there with his stupid, shit-eating grin, went wrong, in the scheme of things?" Caesar asked.

"Where?" Leo asked, using a squeegee to clean the windshield.

"When he decided to be ashamed of his past. The point when he was sitting in his jail cell, just like we did, and he got to thinking one night, lying there in his bunk staring at the ceiling. Maybe it was something the judge said to him, or maybe the prison preacher, or maybe even one of the guards laid a guilt trip on him. Doesn't matter. But somehow the next morning he woke up and changed everything he thought about life. He flipped all his opinions," Caesar said and then grabbed Leo's hand to make him stop cleaning. "He sold out."

"Oh," Leo said, and looked down, certain that if Caesar looked in his eyes right then, he'd know that Leo wasn't far behind the kiss-ass guy.

The two were silent for a moment, listening to the sound of passing interstate traffic.

"Well," Leo ventured, "if he's that weak-minded of a person, and also on account of how that girl got away with it too, don't you think two guys like us are smart enough to add a little bit more onto our gas tab with a little shopping? Since we're planning on paying him back anyway and all."

Caesar thought about it for a moment and concocted a plan in his head.

"Fine whatever. Let's go shopping. Just make it quick. We can't afford to slip up, not after we've come this far. My kid's waiting for his daddy," Caesar said, relishing the word "daddy" as it slid off his tongue.

The two entered the store. The clerk spotted them immediately.

"Afternoon guys! Hot enough for you?" he greeted them cheerfully.

Caesar turned his back on the guy and gritted his teeth, digging his fingernails into his palms, focusing hard on the mental picture of Loretta's belly.

"Howdy," Leo called out grabbing a shopping basket and immediately snatching the teddy bear off the floor.

"You guys gonna pay for that gas?" the clerk said, still smiling.

Caesar remembered some relaxation breathing that a yoga teacher once taught the whole cellblock one Saturday morning. He concentrated on breathing to avoid killing.

"Oh yes sir, we'll get you once we're done our shopping," Leo called out, smiling.

The clerk nodded, satisfied and then busied himself straightening up the magazine display in front of the counter.

A couple rows over from Leo, Caesar picked up a tin of sardines from the shelf.

"Ah, what a beautiful sight!" he sighed.

He ducked down out of sight of the clerk, opened a can, slowly peeled off a sardine and held it in the air before sliding it onto his tongue.

"Boy did I miss *that* smell," Leo said.

Caesar swallowed his sardine quickly.

"You fellas need help finding anything?" the kiss ass guy called out.

"No sir, we're good," Leo called out.

Sir? Caesar looked at Leo.

The clerk frowned and returned to his work, but followed them around his store with his eyes just the same. Caesar winked at Leo as a sign to follow his lead. Leo nodded.

"You know Leo, I was reading the bible the other day before we checked out. I tell you, boy were those guards impressed when they saw me, reading the word of God himself. Boy did that show them. You know, that alone should have showed them. I'm as CLEAN as they come," he said loudly.

"Yeah Caesar. You're smarter than all those guys put together," Leo said, but he was distracted.

"Here I am, a man that society has named a criminal, a bad person, reading the word of God himself... when it hits me!" Caesar said, making his way toward the back of the store.

"What hit you?" asked Leo, following.

Caesar pulled Leo into the storage room doorway. For a moment he thought he saw a set of eyes watching him from the darkness inside the room. But then they disappeared.

"I am a messenger," Caesar whispered, grasping Leo's shoulders.

"Like an angel?" Leo asked, awestruck.

"No, better than an angel, like one of God's disciples. I have been given the responsibility to pass on my knowledge and wisdom, and his, to my child," said Caesar loudly, still performing.

"And my godchild," Leo chimed in.

"OK fellas, any time now," the kiss-ass clerk called out, still cheerfully though.

Caesar could tell their borrowed time was running out.

"It's a sign Leo. I tell you it's a sign from God. Why else would I be rotting away in jail this time, only to get that picture in the mail from Loretta? I told you I felt something religious happen during that conjugal visit awhile back!" Caesar said, ignoring the man's glare but walking toward the front of the store nevertheless.

"You did! I remember!" Leo exclaimed, following along and filling the basket.

"This is a blessing. It's my holy duty to pass on my beliefs, my morals… My inner being… To my son," Caesar said.

"And those dumb cops thought we broke out for ourselves! Who do they think they're dealing with?" Leo said, winking at Caesar.

The clerk looked up from the magazine rack.

"They'll see. When I'm done with parenting, every kid in the world will want me to be their father," Caesar said.

"And me their godfather," Leo said.

They arrived at the counter and Leo plopped down the shopping basket overflowing with supplies. He put his hand on the teddy bear protectively. The clerk scanned the items in record time.

"And with the gas that'll be a grand total of $63.57 fellas. Will that be cash or charge?"

Caesar and Leo looked at each other.

"Well?" the clerk said, now holding out his hand, all prior signs of ass kissing wiped clean from his face.

"Leo does this guy look familiar to you?" Caesar asked.

The clerk grimaced and Leo did see something eerily familiar in his eyes.

"Not really Caesar," Leo answered nervously.

"Really? Because I could have sworn he has the look of a guilty man, working real hard to be innocent," Caesar said.

"Cash or charge?" the clerk repeated, now with an edge in his voice.

"And guilty men trying to be innocent generally aren't looking to start any trouble are they Leo?"

"Nah, that seems like that'd be a dumb thing to do Caesar."

The clerk glared at Caesar and Leo.

"We both know you let that pretty girl rip you off earlier." You don't look blind to me. You didn't want to draw attention to the store so you figured no harm no foul," Caesar said and motioned Leo toward a stack of plastic shopping bags behind the counter.

"What the…" the clerk said as Leo grabbed a handful of bags and started bagging the items from their basket.

"Shhhh," Caesar said, pressing his finger to his lips and pointing to the gun shaped bulge in Leo's jumpsuit pocket.

"We both know how this is going to work and there's no need for you to say a single word about it."

He helped Leo finish bagging the items in silence as the clerk watched, breathing heavy with nostrils flared. As they started to walk out the door though, they heard a click behind them. Caesar elbowed Leo and they turned around, hands raised, unsurprised to see the clerk aiming a shotgun at them.

"Drop the bags," the clerk ordered.

"But," Leo said.

"I said drop them!"

The plastic bags crumpled to the floor and their contents rolled all over the dirty scuffed up tile floor. Leo pushed the teddy bear into the corner with his foot.

"You really want to draw attention to yourself over $63 in convenience store crap? Because if you do what you're pretending you wanna do, your life is over and we both know it," Caesar said walking toward the counter.

"Now drop that," the clerk repeated, nodding toward Leo's jumpsuit pocket. Leo looked down at it.

"Go ahead buddy, I'm not worried about this guy," Caesar reassured Leo without turning around or taking his eyes off the clerk.

Leo laid the gun down gently on the floor.

Caesar continued to stare at the clerk, to the point of discomfort.

"Jesus Christ man, what's your problem? I'm the one with the gun! Don't you know when you're beat?" the clerk exclaimed, and then jumped as the entry bell on the door rang and someone started to come in the store.

Leo slammed the full weight of his body against the glass door, forcing the person back outside.

"If your trigger happy little index finger had been a centimeter in a different direction just now this whole thing would have gone from a threat to a promise," Caesar remarked.

The blood drained from the clerk's face.

"Let me ask you man, what was the number one thing you got out of being in jail?" Caesar asked him.

The clerk thought about it.

"I know for me, it was the power of repentance. Everyone gets a second chance you know? For instance, Leo and I got locked up because we didn't have a purpose. There we were running around trying to save people from their own worst demons and make them better citizens. But we had no end goal, you know? But now I'm going to be a father, and Leo a godfather," Caesar said.

"That's right," Leo chimed in.

"Now—we have an even bigger reason to clean up the world. A second chance. For my son," Caesar finished. "What about you?"

"The number one thing I got out of jail," the clerk said, "was lost. Even more lost than I was when I went in. At least I thought I had a plan before I went in. When I got out, suddenly I didn't have a plan. Nobody told me what I was supposed to do. I've been lost ever since. I don't know who I am."

"And now all you've got is this job," Caesar said.

"Yeah."

"And if you decide to blow our heads off, you get to go back in," Caesar said.

Leo crouched down and picked the gun back up.

"Hey, what do you think you're doing!" the clerk demanded, coming back to life.

"I don't think you really wanna go back in," Leo said putting the gun back in his pocket. "I think if you go back in you'll end up even more lost. But it will be worse this time because you'll know the difference. This time you'll know you had a choice. That it didn't have to end this way."

"Keep your job man. You never know what might come of it. God might have other plans for you yet," Caesar said. "Now I'm going to reach into my pocket but I don't have a gun so I want you to take a deep breath and tell that finger of yours to calm the hell down."

The clerk nodded.

Caesar slid the knife out of his pocket and laid it on the counter.

"Caesar no!" Leo protested.

"Consider this a present from one ex-con to another," Caesar said. "A knife in need of redemption, for a man in need of it too. We square now?"

"As long as you both get out and never come back. Ever," the clerk said bitterly.

Caesar nodded, and he and Leo scooped as many of the items on the floor as he could back into the plastic bags and walked out the door.

After Leo exited, with one hand on the front door Caesar looked back at the clerk.

"I've been missing it lately too," he told him.

"What?" the clerk asked.

"The safety. Predictability. Routine. Even the strictest rules. Being locked up had its perks you know? In a lot of ways it's the most secure I ever felt in my whole life," Caesar said, clutching his stomach as if he'd been punched.

"Do the rest of us a favor then and go the hell back," the clerk said, glaring across the counter at Caesar.

Caesar tried to get the words out, all of them, but the acid had risen up his throat again and all that came out was a juicy belch.

"Still wonder why we are the way we are Leo?" Caesar asked Leo bitterly as he joined Leo back at the car.

Leo was silent.

"Because if we didn't have something to live for, we'd end up like that, a broken man living in a state of permanent shame," said Caesar adding, "which is, Leo, the most crippling emotion a man can feel."

A minute later, roaring down the highway in the Camaro, Leo sifted through the plastic shopping bags in his lap.

They passed another sign warning motorists of a nearby state prison.

"Caesar, I've always wondered why do they keep all the prisons in the desert?" Leo asked.

"Keeps the bad seeds away from society. That's why we're heading for the country Leo. I don't want my kid getting messed up with the scum we just left behind," Caesar responded.

"So Loretta knows we're coming? I thought you couldn't find her?" Leo asked.

"I couldn't. But I think we'll make for a nice surprise," Caesar said.

"You're real good at surprises," said Leo.

"The best. Besides, what kind of mother wouldn't want her baby to have his dad around?" Caesar said.

"We're all gonna be one big happy family, you and Loretta and the baby and me. He's gonna be the luckiest kid around to have so many people loving him," Leo's said.

"It'll be just like a storybook, right buddy?" Caesar said.

Silence.

"Leo? What is it?" Caesar asked his distracted friend.

"I don't know. I get the feeling I forgot something," Leo said, continuing to sift through the bags.

Caesar looked down at the seemingly endless dirt ribbon of highway in front of them and then in the side rearview at the same behind them.

"We got enough supplies. That's all we need," he told Leo.

"Yup. Definitely missing something."

This time it was Leo who wasn't listening. He bit his lip and looked down at the plastic bags. Suddenly he jumped up in his seat.

"What the hell's wrong with you?" Caesar demanded.

"The teddy bear!" Leo shouted.

"Not a teddy bear—what the hell's wrong with YOU Leo!" Caesar yelled.

Leo pointed back down the road toward the store excitedly.

"I forgot the teddy bear! I found this teddy bear that I wanted to give to the baby. Caesar it was perfect!"

"Shut up! Forget the teddy bear. Give me a break!" Caesar yelled.

"No! I have to get the teddy bear! How am I gonna look to the family, huh? I don't want my own god baby to hate me!" Leo yelled.

"My son will hate whoever he wants to hate!" Caesar fired back.

"Not me! Not if we go back and get him the teddy bear. Come on..." Leo argued.

"Settle down!" Caesar ordered and sped up.

"Our baby needs to know how much I love him. He needs to know what a loving, decent person I am!" Leo yelled.

Caesar didn't see how he was going to get out of this, or at the very least how he would get Leo to stop shouting in his ear. He slowed down a little to think.

"What are you trying to do to me buddy?" he muttered.

"I'll just be a minute Caesar. I promise," Leo said.

"What about Mr. Trigger Happy and his shotgun, not to mention Jim's knife? You really want to give him a chance to change his mind? I was trying to let the son of a bitch redeem himself—for Jim!" Caesar said.

"I'll sneak in! Or even better, I'll bribe a tourist to grab it off the floor where I left it!" Leo insisted.

"Bribe? With what? We're outta money in case you forgot!" Caesar said.

"I'll give 'em some of our supplies," Leo said.

"Are you forgetting Caesar's commandment..."

"I know, never go back to the scene of a crime Caesar, especially your own. But how many things have I ever asked you for?" Leo said.

"You're making me stupid Leo. You're making me plain stupid," Caesar said as he peeled into a U-turn and sped back toward the store.

But with the corner of his mouth pulling back into a small smile he murmured, "For a teddy bear. For a goddamn teddy bear!"

"Not for a teddy bear," Leo corrected him, "To make sure your kid gets a better start than we did."

CHAPTER EIGHT
MAN DOWN

Behind the store, Caesar cut the engine, put the car in neutral, and both men quietly got out, pushing the Camaro the rest of the way to the back door of the convenience store. Caesar pointed at the door, propped open with a brick.

"Make it quick," Caesar said, looking anxiously around for any signs of anything.

"I will Caesar. Don't worry. This will all be good," Leo said calmly, patting the gun in his pocket.

Then he slipped stealthily into the back door of the store, each footstep quieter than the last. Leo pretended he was nothing but a ghost sliding invisibly back into the scene of a crime that happened centuries ago.

Caesar waited in the car, his heart pounding and hands trembling. Shit, he wouldn't be this wound up if only Leo let him take care of this. This was like waiting for a baby to be born without a cigar to chomp on. The air around him was sweltering. Sweat dripped from his temples down to his chin. Invisible hands were closing around his throat. This was torture. He couldn't wait a moment longer. Caesar got out of the car and walked to the back door of the store. He had his hand on the door handle when the door flew open, almost knocking him over.

"It's about damn time!"

Caesar's heart sank. It wasn't Leo. It was the teenage girl he and Leo had watched shoplifting earlier. She wasn't much happier to see him. She also didn't look properly scared. She was worn out and irritated, with far too much wear and tear on her face for a young girl.

As soon as Tonya recognized Caesar she attempted to retreat back inside. But Caesar's arm was already around her neck.

"You've got it all wrong," she said calmly.

"Like hell I do, you're in on it with that piece of shit weasel in there! You were setting us up earlier weren't you?"

"No I wasn't I swear! I was still gathering my stuff up and… seeing what else he had back here. I lost track of time and then your friend suddenly walked by me back into the store. I could hear him clip clopping all the way through the store but, but none of that matters now because that guy's gonna kill him. He's gonna kill your friend," Tonya said breathlessly.

"That's what I was comin' out here to tell you. I guessed you might be out here waiting for him," she finished breathlessly.

Caesar saw in her eyes that she was telling the truth. He knew that because it was the first time he'd ever seen honesty in a woman's eyes. He had wanted his mother to be telling the truth when she promised she'd quit screwing other guys, and he'd wanted Loretta to be telling the truth when she said she'd keep visiting him every week until he finally got out of prison and they could be together again.

Caesar didn't want to believe her. But this was Leo she was talking about, the only person in the world worth doing something this stupid.

Caesar nudged the girl back into the store.

"If you make so much as a peep you're dead, I'll kill you with my bare hands," he whispered to her.

Tonya nodded. The two stood in the storeroom doorway and Caesar peeked around the corner at the front of the store. The clerk had Leo pinned against the wall behind the counter, pushed against a gigantic clear plastic storage bag bulging with rolls of toilet paper. Leo's own .45 was shoved into his chest. He looked scared and somewhat bewildered at what was going down and kept losing his footing and sliding down the plastic bag onto the floor. After a few too many slides, the clerk finally flung his elbow across Leo's neck, propping him up against the wall like a flailing wooden marionette.

"Owwww," Leo moaned as the clerk pushed the handgun even harder into his sternum.

He struggled to say more, but his captor tried to crush his windpipe and all that came out was a gurgle.

The clerk, Caesar could tell by looking at his face, had snapped. He was cashing in his one-way ticket back to the safety and sureness of prison. He was a completely different man than the one they'd left here less than an hour ago.

Caesar noticed that Jim's knife was still on the counter, exactly where he'd left it next to the register. The shotgun was nowhere in sight. Sneaking steadily closer to the front of the store behind displays and store aisles, Caesar finally got a good enough view to see the teddy bear dangling by Leo's side. He had a death grip on the damn thing.

"All for a goddamn bear," he sighed.

"That's all he tried to take when he came in. I thought I was seeing things," the girl whispered over his shoulder.

"What the hell are you doing here?" he hissed through his teeth.

Tonya placed her index finger to her lips and ducked lower.

She looked serious, even invested in the situation, and he couldn't figure out why. He could tell she wasn't legitimately afraid of him. She could have easily hung back in the storeroom and then fled the moment he entered the store. Caesar felt the situation slipping out of his control. He dug his fingers into her upper arm. She was unfazed.

Behind the counter the clerk pushed his elbow deeper into Leo's neck but the sweat made it slip off.

"Please," Leo whispered, gasping for air for a moment.

"You're my hostage until that other son of a bitch comes back to claim you," the clerk said, putting his elbow back on Leo's neck.

Caesar saw how much he was enjoying this. He recognized the excited tremor in the guy's voice and the anger blazing in his eyes. He was playing with his prey and loving every moment of it. Caesar suddenly noticed how quiet it was outside. Fear gripped him in his gut. He realized that nobody had called the cops. Society had gotten so selfish and lazy, Caesar realized, that minding your own business was now an art form.

There would be no chance of rescue. And worse yet he didn't know what the hell he was going to do with young Bonnie here once everything went down the way it inevitably would. He felt strangely protective of her.

He looked up and saw tears rolling down Leo's face. Caesar could feel his fear. The hairs on his arm stood up and he felt nauseous. He'd never seen Leo so terrified, even during their very worst jobs and all the shit that happened in that prison. Caesar truly believed that this madman was going to kill Leo—and not in a reasonable, polite way either.

Turning blue and clearly delirious, Leo made a weak-grasping effort for the gun.

"Damn it Leo," Caesar groaned.

Caesar's suspicions about the clerk's cruel intentions were confirmed when he lowered the .45 and blasted a quarter-sized hole in Leo's left thigh.

Blood gushed from the ragged hole in the jumpsuit. Caesar squeezed his eyes shut, physically unable to handle what would surely come next. He had seen enough gunshot wounds (hell, he was usually on the trigger end) to know the guttural yell of pain that came next—primal, like a wounded animal.

Leo howled and Caesar felt his heart break.

"What's your friend doing?" Tonya whispered, nudging his elbow.

For a brief moment, Caesar panicked, thinking that perhaps the bullet had really gone into Leo's chest and not his thigh. He forced himself to open his eyes and look again. Leo was gazing deep into the hole in his own thigh, watching the blood gush out and run down the creases in the plastic bag like little rivers.

What Leo saw in that hole was the dining room table and the bullet hole in his father's chest that his mother had just delivered. He always wondered if his father had felt pain. Unfortunately, this didn't answer his question. Leo knew the pain was there. He felt the sting of the bullet entering his thigh at close range, tearing through muscle, nerves and bone. As the blood continued to pour out, he knew that the pain was probably awful, more awful than he ever could have imagined. But he was already drifting away from it, like it was a dream. He looked up and suddenly saw Caesar crouched behind the store shelves, gaping at him with worried eyes. The same worried eyes he himself had looked through that day, sitting at the dining room table. He tried to smile and wave at Caesar to reassure him but he couldn't lift his arm. It also seemed like it would take a monumental effort to work his face muscles. He tried to communicate using his eyes.

Crouched by the shelves, Caesar saw that Leo's eyes were no longer worried. It was probably wishful thinking on his part, but they seemed to be smiling at him. He shook his head and refocused on the task at hand—rescuing his best friend. But the clerk was determined to make that impossible.

Unsatisfied with Leo's complacent reaction to what was supposed to be the worst kind of physical torture, he reloaded the handgun, aimed, and blasted a hole into Leo's right leg. Clothing, skin, tissue, muscle and arteries all tore once again and the blood gushed like a volcano, but Leo's face remained unchanged. The clerk knew he wasn't dead because he was still blinking and breathing and his eyes were flicking around, uncontrolled.

The clerk was now panting and sweating profusely from the hardest charge of adrenaline he'd felt in years. He was giddy. All his carefully orchestrated efforts to be a normal, hard working, clock punching citizen were now splattered all over the floor and wall in front of him.

"That's right buddy. I'm going limb by limb until your coward of a friend comes back for you," he told Leo.

Leo's eyes swiveled forward from where they'd been looking off into the distance and regarded his captor calmly.

"Son of a bitch, he's not your buddy," Caesar whispered to himself.

"What are we gonna do?" someone whispered back.

He had forgotten that Tonya was still beside him.

"You've now had two good opportunities to escape," he heard himself say.

"I thought you might need my help," she said.

"I can handle this," Caesar said.

He noticed Leo's eyes kept falling shut.

"Use me," Tonya said.

"I can't. You're innocent," he said.

"So you think," she said matter-of-factly.

Leo was as white as the toilet paper in the plastic bag. If Caesar was in his right mind he would have known his buddy was as good as dead. But the only words in his head that he could make out were, "I can't let him die."

He got down on his hands and knees and prepared to make a move. Leo, ever his loyal and trained partner, opened his eyes enough to see what Caesar was doing. Summoning every bit of strength in his body, Leo let out an animal howl, giving Caesar the cover he needed to race to the counter, and grab the knife while the clerk was distracted.

Tonya watched from her hiding place looking at him. *Now what?*

Caesar had no idea what the answer was but he knew he'd better think fast because Leo was fading fast.

"Psst," Tonya whispered softly.

He looked over. She held a jar full of jelly in the air and Caesar saw her plan immediately. He scooted over to the edge of the counter, readied the knife and nodded at Tonya.

CRASH!

She smashed the jelly jar into the floor as hard as she could. As the impact vibration traveled around the store, sticky shards of thick red glass sprayed all over the store aisle.

At the same time, the clerk leapt to his feet firing the .45 blindly in the direction of the noise, howling like a madman. Fortunately Tonya was already low crawling as fast as she could back toward the storeroom, out of sight.

Caesar counted the bullets as they fired and did the mental math, subtracting the ones that were embedded in his best friend's body. He knew the clip was empty before the clerk realized it. He also knew that the clerk had completely lost control and was operating on pure paranoia. He moved into position. Knife outstretched, Caesar was about to lunge when the clerk turned and spotted him crouching on the floor by the register.

"Motherfu..." the clerk bellowed.

But in his paranoia, he made a critical mental error and didn't realize he was pulling the trigger on an empty gun. As the empty gun clicked at Caesar, he charged, knife outstretched, thrusting it deep into the clerk's gut. As a kid, hungry for knowledge and having an urgent daily need to hide from his home life, Caesar would steal and stockpile books from the local library, reading voraciously for hours after school. One of those books was *Grey's Anatomy*. He knew exactly where to find the intersection of major arteries in the clerk's gut. Once he was in there and the clerk's arms and legs went limp from the shock of the attack, he angled the knife upward.

"Caesar's commandment number eight—never lose focus."

Then he watched in awe as the life drained out of his fellow ex-con.

"Coward," he said, looking down in disgust at the gutted fish.

He thought of the old lady in the bank.

"Rest in peace Arthur. Give my regards to Jim."

As he looked down at the knife, Caesar suddenly remembered how he'd really acquired it. He and Leo had been crouching behind the dumpster outside the bank, feasting on fast food leftovers. It was noontime and the bank parking lot was packed and bustling with well-dressed people, squeezing in their bank errands over lunch hour. He promptly vetoed Leo's bank robbery idea and as they got up to leave, he made one last pass of the dumpster, in case they'd missed anything potentially valuable. That's when he spotted the bloodstained knife lying on the bottom, discarded evidence from someone else's mission. He sent Leo in to fetch it.

"Caesar... the teddy bear," Leo mumbled incoherently, pulling Caesar out of his trance and back into the convenience store bloodbath.

Caesar looked down and saw that his buddy was trying to push the teddy bear, still gripped tightly in his hand, toward him.

Leo's breathing was growing even shallower, his skin ashen, with eyes glazed over but still open and staring. He blinked up at Caesar pushing the teddy bear into him.

The damn teddy bear again. A cheap cotton stuffed toy. The state of Arizona on its little red shirt was soaked through with the blood of the childlike man who wanted nothing more than to present it to his godchild. And now he was going to die for the damn thing.

Caesar suddenly heard the sound of the Camaro starting, and then driving away through the gravel behind the store. He contemplated this for a moment, listening as the engine got quieter and quieter as the car got further and further away, along with the mysterious girl who had come to his rescue. He still wasn't mad at her. She was playing the same game he was—survival of the fittest.

Meanwhile, Leo was fighting with every last drop of life in his body to keep his eyes open and stare at Caesar. He knew Caesar wasn't going to let him die and it was his job to stay awake to see how he would save him.

He also knew that his mother wouldn't really make him leave that day. She'd been testing him to see how much he loved her. He'd followed along with her instructions, knowing that she would eventually find him and let him know it was safe to come back home.

He just had to stay awake now. But his eyesight was getting so blurry and the room kept spinning around, like this was all a dream. Everything had an echo to it, like it was all happening inside a steel barrel.

So, when Leo heard a bell and saw a blurry figure emerging out of the haze and walking toward them, he thought it was all a part of the same dream.

Alerted by the doorbell, Caesar looked up.

Deeply engrossed with his phone, the twenty-something preppy punk wandered blindly into the horror movie scene.

"You guys sell beer?" the kid mumbled without looking up from his phone.

"Yeah sure," Caesar said, "fridge against the back wall."

Head still down, the kid waved and meandered to the back of the store.

Leo reached up and with one last burst of strength, grabbed Caesar's hand, staring into his eyes. Caesar stared back. Then Leo closed his eyes, and that was it.

Caesar made the sign of the cross over himself, kissed his fingers and touched Leo's forehead. He ground his teeth together until his head hurt. He wanted to kill the clerk again and now he wanted to kill this punk for sabotaging his last moment with Leo.

A six-pack of beer bottles slapped onto the counter, followed by...

"Holy shit."

The clueless young guy finally tore himself away from his gadget long enough to see the carnage. Caesar stood up, realizing he was standing in a pool of the blood of two fellow ex-cons—a shit bag and a saint. He looked down and saw that he was decorated from head to toe with splatters of blood. He and the kid locked eyes. Caesar clenched his fists by his sides and realized that the bloody knife was still in his hand. The preppy kid froze, trapped in a moment of terror and disbelief. Caesar realized from his reaction that this was the first real moment the kid had ever experienced in his life. He stood frozen at the counter, one hand on his phone, the other with a death grip on the six-pack waiting for instructions.

"Never bring beer to a knife fight son," Caesar told him.

The kid started to hyperventilate as Caesar started walking toward him with the knife.

The kid screamed, dropped the beer on the floor and fled the store. Caesar started to chase him but slid first in the blood and then the beer, lunging for the counter to break his fall. He took it as a sign from God that this particular piece of shit punk wasn't supposed to die today. Besides, enough blood had already been shed, Caesar reasoned. He was officially in mourning. All he wanted to do was get out of there and find some space to clear his head.

Caesar knew there was nothing else to do but go. He couldn't bring himself to look at Leo's face one last time. He needed to remember his best friend looking up hopefully at him, blinking, about to say something else. It was the readiness and hope for something better, always so present in Leo that would leave the largest and emptiest hole in Caesar's heart.

His eyes fixated on the ceiling, he tore the teddy bear from Leo's hand and found a cleaning cloth under the counter that he used to wipe the blood off the knife and return it to his pocket. Then he dabbed the blood off the teddy bear the best he could. Caesar stopped and listened for a minute for sirens. Nothing, of course. None of the cast of characters from the desert tragedy he'd just survived had anything to gain by involving the cops. Everyone was in it for himself or herself.

He reached up and touched his father's dog tags around his neck. He considered draping them around Leo's neck as a tribute.

"You would've liked Leo, Dad. He was loyal to me until the moment he died. And he never once stopped trying to make me an honest man," Caesar said.

He paused, tightly gripping the metal in his hand.

"I might be sentimental but I'm not stupid enough to leave ID at the scene of a crime."

He walked out from behind the counter and executed a rapid fire shopping spree, gathering everything he could including a set of souvenir clothing. He crammed it all into a canvas bag embroidered largely with "I heart Arizona."

As he left, he scooped up the empty .45 and dropped it in the bag.

He jogged out through the storeroom through the back of the store out to the parking lot. It didn't occur to him until he stepped foot in the gravel lot that he had no way of getting the hell out of there. Crazy Bonnie had taken his wheels. He reminded himself that he would have done the same thing in her situation. She was the first woman he'd ever met who seemed to operate like he did. He marveled at that while walking around the side of the store with the bloody teddy bear in one hand and the bag in the other. He hoped for a moment that the stupid kid would still be out front; that would solve the problem of revenge and transportation.

But the front parking lot was as empty as the land for miles around. Off in the distance, cars whizzed by on the interstate, hurrying to the more desirable exit as fast as they could, as if they knew what had just happened at this exit, where the ramp downhill descended into a sizzling crater of lost souls. The sweltering sun and swirling, clouds of gritty sand slicing at his face also seemed to be in on the torture.

He wished for a car, another person, the kid, the girl, for Leo to miraculously wake up and come walking out the front door—anything to push away the thoughts that were threatening to crush him. He looked solemnly at the front door of the store. The pain was building up, traveling up from where it was born in his gut, making its way up his throat. He was going to explode.

Caesar flung his arms out at his sides and screamed at the top of his lungs. The scream involved every square inch of his body and soul and lasted for a lifetime. If any humans had witnessed it, they would have gotten lost in the intensity and ugliness of the scream. They would have been embarrassed and quickly looked for a solution to the situation to make it stop. The animals who heard it, however, understood. This was the kind of deep, primal pain that words provided no defense against.

Up until now, Caesar always had a plan—somewhere to go, something to work toward, something to say, and someone to say it to. There was always something. Now he stood nowhere with nothing to do and nobody to do it with. He would have preferred the cowardly clerk to come back to life and start shooting at him. That would be something to do. This was unbearable. This was the first time Caesar had been alone with his thoughts since he had met Leo. But then he remembered Loretta and the baby, and forced his legs back into motion. Although now, for the first time, guilt and grief clung to him, weighing down each step forward toward the interstate. He stopped under the overpass to change his clothes on his way to blend back in with civilization, cramming the bloody gas station jumpsuit behind some rocks. As he started moving again, making his way up the off ramp, the revving of an engine grew closer and closer behind him. He stopped walking and turned around as Bonnie—that damn girl again—pulled the Camaro over to him and motioned for him to get in.

"What are you playing at?" he asked her.

"Nothing. I just decided it wasn't worth it for you to make me into a full-fledged thief so I've been circling around looking for you," she answered.

"Just one in training right?" Caesar asked.

She ignored him.

"OK if you're not a thief, why are you driving my car?" he asked still standing next to it.

"This is your car?" her eyes bore through him worse than the sun.

"Yes. I won it fair and square," he said.

"They're coming for you. Maybe not yet, but eventually someone's going to get desperate, pull in looking for a bathroom and some turkey jerky, and they're gonna find the bodies. And your DNA is all over that store," she said without emotion, staying put in the driver's seat.

"Yeah, I know," he said, "and this [indicating the passenger seat] is my only choice."

"Take it or leave it," Tonya said, gunning the engine.

Caesar climbed into the passenger seat, thinking the whole time that Leo was the last person to sit there. Caesar had nothing to say and rode silently beside a woman.

Tonya took the hint and kept quiet too. She was well aware that this guy still most likely had at least one weapon on him. She hadn't been lying when she said she came back to pick him up because she wasn't a thief (even though she knew damn well the car wasn't his; he didn't care about it like a regular possession). But she hadn't told this Caesar guy the real reason why she was secretly glad they had both been in that store at the same time. Tonya knew this guy as much as she knew herself.

They were both running from bad memories that they had only partially caused, but were in danger of getting trapped under if they didn't get the hell away. Tonya maxed out the speedometer on the old car, praying that the engine wouldn't self-destruct as the unlikely pair of outlaws motored down the road.

CHAPTER NINE
ROTTEN

Minutes later, off to the side of the shiny, coveted travel plaza down the interstate, Caesar checked the air pressure in the car's tires. Tonya had offered but he shooed her into the building to use the little girl's room and get them some hot food. The thought of even another bite of jerky or bag of chips turned Caesar's stomach.

He didn't know why he was keeping her around other than the fact that she seemed useful, had some cash, and was a completely fascinating creature to him. He felt obligated to despise her a certain amount just for being a woman, but since she wasn't acting like one, it confused him. He also kept trying not to notice that Tonya was incredibly attractive and even sexy. He still didn't know how old she was, but he suspected that any decent gambler would have bet the under on whether she was legal.

He tried not to watch the swing of her hips as she strolled over and handed him a greasy bag of fast food that smelled like salty heaven and the chocolate milkshake he'd specifically requested. He was impressed that she'd gotten his order right, but still annoyed at how she continued to study him like a science project.

"Stop looking at me like that," he snapped, opening the bag and devouring the contents as fast as he could.

"If you're worried about a positive ID, it's too late, I know what you look like," she said.

"You won't turn me in. Only a complete head case would steal a car, flee the scene of a crime, come back and offer a person a ride only to turn on them," Caesar said.

"How do you know if I'm a complete head case or not?" she asked.

"Lucky guess," he said, slurping the milkshake as loud as he could to shut her up.

"Now what?" she asked, motioning toward the car.

"Now, I'll take over the driving," he said.

"Hold on, what makes you think I want to keep traveling with you indefinitely?" she said, acting offended.

Caesar tossed his head back and laughed. Maybe she was a complete head case after all.

"Don't you dare laugh at me!"

Now she was just pissed.

"What's your other option, sweetheart? Thumbing a ride in hopes of getting the attention of a nice new daddy figure who will take you home and make you his little pet? If I was going to do anything to you it would've already been done. Let's just admit that we need each other—or at least that we can help each other out some—and get outta here," Caesar said adding, "Besides Bonnie, you're a witness don't forget. I'm sure your prints are in that store somewhere too and we're both probably on candid camera."

"I," she said fiercely, poking her finger into her chest to make the point, "don't need anyone! Especially a loser who couldn't even keep his best friend alive!"

Caesar's mind went blank and the world started to spin. He wanted to hurt this girl and protect her from him at the same time. He hurled the car keys at her face, right in her stupid, searching, smart eyes. But her well-conditioned street reflexes were lightning fast. Her hand shot out and grabbed the keys right before they made contact.

"Take the car, you lousy thief! I was done with it anyway," he said, turning and walking away before she could argue.

The damn thing only reminded him of Leo anyway, he reasoned.

He walked toward the travel plaza. In a busy place like this he'd have no problem finding another ride. But he knew that young two-faced Tonya wouldn't be able to reconcile her morality as easily.

Eventually she'd realize that she not only watched a murder but now she was aiding the murderer. Caesar wondered why the idea of wrongdoing, but not actual wrongdoing, struck such a nerve with her. He was tempted to turn back around and see if she still out in the parking lot, to go ask her, but then her words rang in his ears again, "couldn't even keep his best friend alive."

"Fuck 'er."

He heard her rev the Camaro's engine and peel out of the parking lot behind him as he walked through the automatic sliding doors into the refreshing chill of the building.

Caesar tried to shut himself down again, something he'd been trying to do since watching Leo die. He followed his own commandment and forcefully pulled his mind out of the mix, switching to autopilot.

Never lose focus.

He was usually good at this but today he felt like there was someone following him wherever he went.

He sat on a bench in the middle of the travel center, with the souvenir canvas bag wedged between his shins on the floor, an elaborately tiled mosaic of earth tones that made him dizzy. He looked up, scanning the place, and scoping out a ride. Soon, the hot greasy meal caught up with him and Caesar let out a grunt, grabbed his gut and ran for the restroom. He camped out in a stall and emptied his guts, groaning with the most pleasure he'd felt in awhile. Pleasure turned to sleepiness and then, the exhaustion of his recent life finally caught up with him and he started to doze off, right there on the crapper. When he looked up Leo was standing over him in his blood-drenched gas station jumpsuit.

"How did I die Caesar?" Leo asked.

"I don't remember exactly."

It wasn't really a lie since Caesar's brain, in survival mode, had already converted memories of the incident into fuzzy images.

"Then maybe I'm not dead. Did anyone check?" Leo asked.

"Yeah, I checked. That piece of shit clerk..." Caesar trailed off, looking away.

"What clerk?" Leo asked blankly.

"What do you mean what clerk? Where'd you come from anyway?" Caesar asked suspiciously.

"Hell and back," Leo said rather cheerfully.

"Smart ass," Caesar retorted with a smile.

"You weren't going to go and do this without me, were you?" asked Leo.

"I can't look out for you every minute Leo. Eventually you're gonna have to be responsible for yourself," Caesar said.

Leo laughed heartily.

"What the hell are you laughing at?" snapped Caesar.

"Nothing Caesar. Let's just get on with this. I don't have all day," said Leo.

"Let's get on with… what, incidentally?" Caesar asked him.

Leo pressed a finger to his lips and motioned to listen. Caesar's head jerked up and he realized he was still sitting on the crapper, drooling into his folded arms.

A young guy talking on his cell phone had entered the restroom.

"I'm telling you man, it freaked me out. I've never seen one dead body before let alone two. The tall guy up against the wall laying on the toilet paper… It was almost funny," the kid said.

Caesar's ass was a lead weight, glued to the toilet seat by gravitational force. It was the punk from the store. He recognized the kid's carefree, entitled voice. What he saw in the store was something that happened—but it didn't happen to him.

"Man, between the two of them there was so much blood I had to run out of there before I surfed out, you know?" he laughed, but Caesar didn't buy his act for a minute.

What he saw had scared the living shit out of this kid. Nevertheless, Caesar could feel adrenaline pumping through his body more and more with every sarcastic, surfer boy-sounding, casual word that spewed forth from the kid's perfectly straight, white-toothed mouth. As he pondered the cruelty of life that this piece of shit was alive and Leo was dead, his face flushed hot and his ears began to ring. He was so distracted by his thoughts, that he barely noticed that the kid had changed the subject.

"Nah, my old man doesn't know where I am. Why, do I sound like I give a shit?" the ungrateful little asshole bragged. "Nothing I ever do is good enough for him so I've given up trying. It's not worth the work, you know what I mean?"

Caesar didn't know what he meant. He couldn't imagine what this kid's father was asking of him that wasn't worth the work. He smelled surfer boy's uselessness like a pheromone; he was a breather doing nothing but wasting precious space that Leo could be occupying, or his son could. Although he had the urge to bust out of the stall, whip out his knife and gut the kid like a stinking fish, Caesar saw the image of a bumper sticker he and Tonya had seen on a mini-van, scrolling repetitively through his mind: *What would Jesus do?* And since he couldn't think of a decent answer to the question, he took some deep breaths, wiped up, and looked around the stall for Leo but there was no sign of him.

He heard the kid finally hang up ("catch you later dude" or some shit like that). As he exited the stall carrying his souvenir bag, Caesar decided that even Jesus himself would want this kid dead. Caesar looked him over for the first time. Back in the convenience store he'd only had a vague impression, a blonde ghost gripping a six-pack of beer. Now the ghost had materialized into a three-dimensional being. The tanned and tousled brat with a turquoise shark tooth necklace leaned over the sink and splashed water over his face. When he rose up, he saw Caesar in the mirror, standing behind him, leering. Caesar looked in the mirror and saw Leo standing next to him. Leo made a trigger motion with his fingers aimed at the kid.

"Oh SHIT!" the kid cried out, and tried to bolt out of the restroom.

"Shut up!" Caesar demanded, grabbed the kid by his neck and shoved him back into the stall he'd just left.

"Oh SHIT," the kid said, this time, dry heaving from the stench Caesar had left behind.

"Five bucks says this kid's never taken a decent crap in his life, right Caesar?"

Caesar looked up and saw Leo leaning in overhead from the adjacent stall, a big mischievous grin on his face.

"Since when are you a comedian?" he asked him.

"Since I got nothin' to worry about anymore," Leo told him.

"What are you talking about dude?" surfer boy exclaimed and tried to push his way out of the stall but Caesar pushed him into the wall hard.

"Nobody's talking to you yet son," Caesar said.

"I'm not your son," the kid said.

"Can you believe this guy?" Caesar asked Leo, reaching into his back pocket and whipping out the knife.

The kid looked like he was going to piss his pants.

"Not such a cocky punk now, are ya' sport?" Caesar said.

Surfer dude suddenly grew some brain cells and shut his mouth.

"Now, be a good boy and stay put," Caesar instructed and held the knife a few inches from the kid's heart.

"You know who I am?" Caesar asked.

"You were at the store, with those dead guys," the kid stammered.

The tip of the knife moved an inch closer to the kid's heart.

"Gimme a break man, if you wanted to kill me I'd be dead by now," the kid said breathlessly, his chest heaving up and down, and sweat stains making their way through his soft cotton designer t-shirt with a smiley faced stick figure waving enthusiastically from a beach chair.

"Where'd you learn that, on one of those crime TV shows? Is that what you think this is? A scene with a happy ending?" Caesar laughed.

"What do you want, man? I promise to keep my mouth shut if that's what you're worried about!"

"Yeah, you sounded real good at that a few minutes ago! You're a regular goddamn mute!" Caesar said.

"I'm sorry man, I promise I'll shut up," the kid insisted.

"Shut the hell up," Caesar said and nodded at the door.

They listened as someone entered the bathroom, pissed, and then left without washing his hands. Marty started to open his mouth but Caesar wagged a warning finger. The restroom door slammed shut and surfer dude became desperate.

"If you're gonna kill me then let's just get it over with, I can't take this," he said a squirming, suffocating fish with a hook gouged through his cheek.

"Nah, I haven't decided if that's the best use for you yet," Caesar said.

Surfer dude wrinkled up his face like he might cry but then thought better of it and controlled himself.

Caesar looked up and saw Leo still hovering.

"What's your name anyway?" Caesar asked the kid.

"Marty, Marty Slate-"

"Shut up. I didn't ask your family name. As far as you and I are concerned, we don't have families. You could have ended up as a cum stain on someone's mattress. We all could have. But for whatever damn reason, God decided to finish the job. Lucky you. Now you and I are here having a conversation about what's going to happen next, and I just need something to call you," Caesar cut him off.

"I know what you should call him," Leo suggested from up above.

"What? Douchebag? What do you think I should call him Leo?" Caesar looked up and asked him.

Marty followed Caesar's line of vision and stared at the empty space above the toilet stall. His eyes widened and his breathing got faster.

"Oh shit…" he whispered, his eyes darting around wildly.

Caesar continued staring up at Leo.

"I saw a dead cat once when I was little, in the woods behind my house. Its eyes were crusted open, just staring at the sky," Marty said.

"He's not dead!" Caesar shouted.

"Who's not dead? Your buddy from the store?" Marty said quickly.

Before the emotion could even register on his face or Marty knew what was coming, the knife had moved from his heart to his jugular, so close that if he so much as took a breath too deep, he'd be cut.

"Say that again you little prick. Say it again," Caesar said fiercely to the brat.

Marty tried to speak and Caesar moved the knife back to the kid's heart.

"You got nothing to worry about. Chill man!" Marty said breathlessly.

"I'm not worried. I've already decided that you'll make a good hostage. You're not that bright, by the sounds of it you've only got drinking buddies who might miss you and you're not much more than a breather," Caesar said.

"The hell you're taking me hostage! I'm not goin' out like that. You're talking to people that aren't here. You're the dumb one, not me," Marty said, trying to prove what an annoying hostage he would make.

He also remembered some story for chicks he'd read online, telling them how if they're attacked, they should do everything they can to avoid changing locations.

Caesar slugged Marty hard across the jaw and pushed him into the filthy, wet space between the toilet and the wall.

"Wait a minute!" Marty said, shaking with fear.

Caesar recognized with satisfaction the convulsive tremble of a man who finally believed he was going to die. Now he could make some progress.

"Shut up!" Caesar said, cementing his power over the situation.

"Is Leo here?" he asked the brat.

There was dead silence except for Marty's rapid breathing. He nodded and looked up at the space over the stall where Caesar had been looking. The two stared at each other.

"Get up," Caesar said quietly.

Marty stood, trying to wipe the filth of the stall floor off him.

"OK. Listen up, I got a new plan," Caesar told him.

"What's that?" the brat dared ask, albeit meekly.

He glanced down at the knife that Caesar now held loosely in his hand. Caesar followed his gaze and smirked, tightening his grip around it.

"First of all son, you better get that dumbass idea, out of your head," he said, pushing Marty in front of him out of the stall and sliding the knife into his souvenir bag.

He watched Marty fight to control himself after being called son again.

"I'm gonna need a replacement for Leo for awhile since he keeps disappearing. And now that you know so much about us, it's gonna be you," Caesar said in a casual tone of voice, throwing an arm over Marty's shoulder as they walked through the building out to the parking lot.

"Just because I know what you've done doesn't make me like you," Marty said, frantically trying to make eye contact with any one of the passing tourists. He couldn't get a single one to look in his direction.

"You sound like Leo," Caesar said grinning.

In the middle of the parking lot, the two looked around.

"Weren't you planning on taking me somewhere?" Marty asked slowly.

"Where's your car?" Caesar asked him.

"Are you kidding me? You're kidnapping me in my own car?" Marty asked incredulously.

"Damn straight," Caesar said.

"I could start screaming right now and there'd be ten tourists on you before you could draw your knife," Marty said.

"Once again kid, you've been spending your life watching too much TV and not doin' nearly enough living. You could scream and yell at the top of your lungs right now and all these dumb tourists would do is lower their sheep heads and stare into the sidewalk cracks so deep you'd think the meaning of life was inside. And by time any of them looked up again, your throat would be cut and you'd be lying on the ground dying away," Caesar told him.

"You're a colossal joke man. I don't know what else you've done that you're being chased for, but I get the feeling you're all talk," Marty snapped before turning his back on Caesar and walking to a nearby jeep.

Caesar followed him.

"Leave me alone man. Go crawl under a rock," Marty said, getting in the jeep and starting it.

Caesar bolted around to the passenger side and was seated with the souvenir bag between his legs, aiming the knife at Marty's neck within moments.

"So you're fast, I'll give you that much," Marty said.

He sighed in defeat and backed out of the parking space noting that Caesar was right, every set of eyes at the travel stop was gazing into the sweltering pavement in front of them. Marty felt the beginning twinges of societal disgust but didn't recognize such a complex feeling and chalked it up to heartburn over the situation.

Even as the jeep jostled them over bumps on the interstate, Caesar kept the knife in place and Marty ignored him. Since Marty pulled onto the main road and headed east, he didn't have to correct him.

"So what we have here is a modified hitchhiker situation," Marty said without looking at Caesar.

"We'll see about that," Leo said from the backseat.

Caesar looked in the rearview mirror and saw Leo licking his fingers and dabbing at the gunshot wounds in each thigh.

"Your buddy's back?" Marty asked, looking in the mirror at the backseat.

"You're gonna start with me again?"

Caesar was tired and irritated now that he had to rely on this dumb shit and his jeep to bring him to Loretta and the baby. Having a hostage would help if anyone tried to hassle him. Bouncing down the highway though, he missed his Camaro, and even the girl in it.

"What else should I be doing?" Marty said, moving his neck away from the knife, reaching over Caesar and fishing a pack of cigarettes out of the glove compartment.

"Don't do that," Caesar said as Marty lit one.

"You gonna lecture me on the dangers of an early death?" Marty cracked.

"He's getting too relaxed again Caesar," Leo warned from the back seat.

Cruising down an isolated stretch of highway, Caesar listened out the window for police sirens in the distance but heard none. He wondered who found the bodies and what they did about it. He pictured the store packed with cops, dusting every inch of the place for fingerprints. He saw Leo's hands bound together with zip ties, the body bag zipper being pulled up over his pale, peaceful face. He needed a mental distraction.

"Pull over right here, it's my turn to drive," Caesar said, pointing at an empty stretch of dirt and dried up brush on the side of the interstate.

Marty shrugged, took a drag off the cigarette and blew smoke in Caesar's face.

Kill.

Caesar yanked the steering wheel and sent the jeep barreling into the dirt shoulder. Marty panicked and slammed on the brakes, bringing the jeep to a screeching, swerving stop in a cloud of dust. Caesar reached over and jabbed Marty in his left hand with the knife, drawing a river of blood.

Caesar smiled in satisfaction when Marty's eyes started to get wet.

"Get out NOW!" Caesar yelled.

Grabbing his bleeding hand Marty tumbled out of the jeep and started running along the side of the highway screaming "Help! Help me! Someone!" toward the empty road.

"Another disappointment to tell your daddy about. What a waste of sperm. You would've done better as a stain on the mattress," Caesar yelled, giving chase.

"What do you know about my father?" Marty yelled back, still clutching his hand and running along the shoulder.

"I have a damn good idea what I'd think of you if you were my son," said Caesar, keeping pace.

Physically taxed from the adrenaline, Marty finally stopped and faced Caesar, panting and holding his hand.

"What kind of woman would make a kid for you?" Marty said, urging the conversation forward, hoping to survive by distraction until he could flag down a passing car.

"Why do you want to die so badly?" Caesar asked.

"Why can't you kill me?" Marty asked back, stalling.

"Why do you want to die?" Caesar held his ground.

"I didn't say..."

"Yeah you did," Caesar said.

Marty boldly walked up to Caesar, stopped inches from his face and unleashed the only other weapon left in his arsenal–a temper tantrum.

"You're just like my dad—a coward. Good boy! Good boy! Yes sir, Dad! He just stands there like you, staring at me hoping I'll figure it out! And now a delusional hack of a criminal is finally going to take me out of my misery. Happy times for Marty! You couldn't even keep your friend alive. What kind of father are you?"

"Tell me again that Leo's dead," Caesar said.

"Is he really?" Marty asked.

"Then where is he? Tell me where he is!" Caesar yelled knocking Marty to his knees.

"I don't know man... can we go now? I'll be your hostage, whatever you want, let's just get this over with... you, me, the Leo guy, whatever," Marty whimpered, his head hanging in front of him.

"Are you disrespecting the recently deceased? You haven't earned the right to even say his name! He was ten times the man you could ever dream of being! He was a Goddamn saint! Say his name! Say his name!" Caesar raged, finally letting it sink in that Leo wasn't coming back.

Say my name, say my name! A teenage boy's voice rung in his head.

"Leo, his name was Leo," Marty sobbed in exhaustion.

"You're God damn right it was," Caesar said.

Caesar lunged forward, plunging the knife into the sobbing brat's gut, using the same motion he'd used to execute the kiss-ass clerk. He straddled the jerking and twitching kid, twisting the knife and patiently waiting for him to die, keeping his eyes averted to avoid watching the life drain away as it had from Leo's face. Finally, he heard a gurgle and with one final chest heave—it was over.

Caesar flipped Marty over and pulled the kid's wallet out of his back pocket, smiling at the wad of bills he found in it. He looked at the street address on his tan, smiling driver's license and made a mental note to add Marty's dad to his list of good people he'd pay back someday.

"Good dad, lousy kid," he mumbled.

Then he got in the jeep, dropped the wallet into his bag and drove off, leaving Marty to rot in the desert.

"That's good thinking Leo. We should head away from the highway. I've taught you well," Caesar said a little while later as he pulled the jeep off onto a side road that led deep into the desert.

He grinned at Leo in the rearview mirror.

"Go on. I'm listening," Leo grinned back.

"Hey buddy, might wanna take care of those bullet wounds. They look serious," said Caesar.

Leo ran his hands over his thighs.

"Funny, they don't hurt," he mumbled.

"Pretty messy though," said Caesar.

"I know. I should use club soda," Leo said obediently.

"That's right," Caesar said, checking the sun position to make sure he was still headed in the right direction.

"Do you think she'll be OK?" Leo suddenly asked.

"Who?"

"The girl," Leo answered.

"Don't know," Caesar said.

Leo smiled a knowing smile. Caesar turned around to look at him but Leo was gone again. He frantically searched the jeep and the desert around him but it was getting dark and the shadows started to play tricks on him.

"Leo! Leo! Get back here right now!" he shouted, his voice breaking with desperation.

Even though he was alone in the jeep, such an uncontrolled show of emotion embarrassed him.

CHAPTER TEN
SHOWDOWN

Under a blanket of stars uninterrupted by manmade light, Caesar pulled the jeep off a main dirt road into a small town that seemed to be nothing more than a rest area. With headlights off, he pulled into a ditch out of sight from the road, grabbed the souvenir bag, abandoned the dead kid's jeep, and walked away down the street.

He staked out the small ten-room travel motel while collecting his to-go order from the diner across the street before making the decision to stay for the night. Caesar was sure he saw the tall thin older black man with the kindly eyes and white beard at the front desk give him a knowing look as he checked in. Maybe every dingy room in this shit bag motel had a version of him hiding out in it. He nodded and smiled at the black man as he took his key and left the lobby.

Before turning in for the night, he did several things to reassure himself that everything was normal. He prayed over a Styrofoam container of takeout before eating. After dinner he showered under a weak jet of scorching water, meticulously scrubbing off the grime of the road and hoping some of the memories washed down the rusted motel drain with it. Then he unmade and remade the bed's sagging mattress to meet his standards, auditioned several radio alarm options, set the alarm, turned the light off on the bedside table and went to sleep.

The room was still pitch dark when the sound of someone banging a deck of cards on the table across the room woke Caesar. The cheap lamp dangling over the table flickered on, casting a thin spotlight over a straw head of hair.

Caesar got up and joined Leo at the table, picked up the hand of cards that he'd been dealt and scrutinized it. He saw that the bloodstains on Leo's legs had dried into brown crusty patches. The two quietly engaged in a game of gin rummy. To Caesar's surprise and annoyance, Leo quickly dominated.

"Gin," Leo said, laying down his cards and beaming.

Caesar shuffled and dealt another hand.

"Lucky bastard," he said.

"Only 'cuz of you Caesar."

They continued playing.

"I'll let you win one if you let me be the godfather," Leo said.

"Numbskull, I've told you a hundred times already that you're the godfather. God himself appointed you. Want me to brand it across your chest?" Caesar asked, fiddling with the air controls in the window vent.

Leo looked down at his chest.

"No thanks. Just don't forget again. Your baby needs me," he told Caesar.

"Are you saying I won't be a good enough father?" Caesar asked.

"Hard to tell until I see you with him, or her," Leo said.

"With him. With my son," said Caesar.

"You're sure?"

"Yes. And what do you mean hard to tell? I've done a good job with you haven't I?" asked Caesar.

"I was already more than half a whole person when you got me. He or she is brand new. We gotta be careful or he or she could turn out just like us," Leo said seriously.

"Stop calling my son a girl. Besides, the whole point is to create HIM in our likeness," Caesar said testily.

"There you go again. The same preaching you've been doing forever. And now you want the same for OUR son. You don't care about the slightest possibility that the sinners could be saints and the saints could be..." Leo ranted.

Caesar grinned and laid his hand on the table.

"Gin," he announced triumphantly.

He went to bed shortly after that, trying also to put to bed his fears that the whole card game was a dream. He wished the whole damn day had been a dream. Caesar finally drifted off again, dreaming that he was safely tucked in his prison bunk with the soothing sounds of Leo trying to suck his nose out through his mouth lulling him to sleep from overhead.

The next time Caesar was woken up that night he jerked up angrily in bed, ready to give Leo hell, and found himself looking into the barrel of a gun. The trembling, disheveled young man standing next to his bed motioned to Caesar with the narrow barreled gun to get out of bed.

"On your feet, room number five."

Caesar obliged, climbing out of bed in his t-shirt and boxers, even putting his hands up in the air to help reassure the young fellow. The kid kind of reminded him of Leo so he figured he'd audition him as a new sidekick or at the least, a less mouthy hostage than Marty.

"Are we going for a ride?" he asked.

"Come on! Keep it moving!" the kid ordered, his voice shaking.

Caesar fell in obediently, leading the march out the motel room door toward the parking lot. As the pair arrived outside, the trembling fellow seemed to forget what came next.

"You got a getaway car?" Caesar asked helpfully.

"Yeah! Come on, move it!"

The kid pushed him toward a miniscule, beat-up hatchback. Caesar shook his head in disbelief, squeezed into the passenger seat and buckled the seat belt to set a good example.

"You coming?" he called out the window.

The kid looked around in all directions except at Caesar before getting in and speeding away into the desert night. The tiny hatchback soon slowed to a halt in the dirt, the stars in the sky and headlights serving as the only light.

"Get out, number five."

Caesar unbuckled his seat belt and got out, stretching from the ride as if he were at a rest stop with his family on a cross-country trip.

The fellow walked around the car and pushed Caesar into the headlights. Caesar put his arms up in the air again without being asked.

"Now what?"

"Give me all your money!"

Caesar looked down at his t-shirt and boxers.

"You didn't tell me to bring any," he said.

Still shaking, the kid aimed the gun at Caesar's head.

"Whoa there junior, watch where you aim that thing!"

"Why didn't you? What did you think I wanted?" the kid continued panicking.

"You're the boss. There are many exciting options for a gunman, his prey, and a working automobile in a remote area like this," Caesar said placidly.

"Like what?"

His arms still raised, Caesar leaned casually against the front of the car, crossing his ankles.

"Well robbery is just the tip of the iceberg for an enterprising young man such as yourself. Based on the cleanliness of my underwear you might decide that I'm an important business traveler, temporarily down on my luck, broken down in a seedy motel but nevertheless important enough to demand ransom for."

"Are you?" the kid asked hopefully.

"Nope."

Then Caesar carried on with his lecture.

"Or if you're more into sick, senseless violence for the sake of proving your manhood, there's your standard variety assault, rape, sodomy, and the benefit of a vehicle to move things along nicely."

"Whaddya' mean?"

Caesar got up, lowered his arms and began circling the car. His mind swimming with all kinds of new information, the fellow was too confused to stop him.

"Well Le-... Buddy, this wouldn't be my assault vehicle of choice but you still have options."

He arrived at the driver's side, reached in and put the car in gear. The tiny car began to roll slowly toward the kid who, at that moment was lost in thought, using the gun to rub his temple as he contemplated all the new exciting options for his emerging career. Caesar shook his head in disbelief again. Leo was looking smarter and smarter by the moment.

"Hey kid."

The fellow spun around.

"Three feet to your left," said Caesar.

The kid tried to simultaneously jump out of the way of his own car, aim the gun at Caesar, and cock it. Instead, he forgot to jump, and fell under the front tires, yelling. As he fell, the gun flew out of his hand into the dirt.

"Son of a bitch!" he cried out.

"Well, you would know, wouldn't you son?"

Caesar crouched over the kid's head and scooped up the gun, dangling it just out of his reach. He thought the gun felt light but then again, it was only a 0.22—a chick's gun.

"Commandment number twelve—never drop your gun. Might as well chop off your nuts."

He looked at where the tires had the kid pinned.

"Oh well... that seems to be covered," he laughed.

Sobbing the kid reached for the gun. Caesar paced, furiously lecturing the kid.

"After all I've been through, you woke me up and got me out of bed for this? Kids like you are a complete waste of time and oxygen! At least have a purpose, a reason to own a perfectly decent weapon that I am, of course, going to have to confiscate from you. If for no other reason than to make sure it's put to good use. Something around here needs to fulfill its purpose!"

"I'm sorry man! Don't rape me!" the kid cried out.

"Believe me, what's coming out of this end is hardly impressive to me. I'm pretty damn certain the other end would be even more of a joke," said Caesar.

He cocked the gun and aimed it at the kid's face.

"Now say you're sorry."

"I'm sorry," he whimpered.

Caesar fired. Nothing.

"What the fuck?"

The kid looked away in shame.

"If you knew this thing wasn't loaded what were you trying to pull?" Caesar demanded.

"I need money, man. I need money real bad or my dealer's gonna kill me," the kid whined, sniffling.

Caesar threw his head back laughing.

"And you thought waking up guests like me in that fine negative five star fleabag back there was going to solve this problem for you?" he asked.

"What are you gonna do to me?" the kid pleaded.

Caesar thought about it for a minute, staring up at the clear, star-filled desert sky.

"Well if I'm the judge, jury and executioner and it's between you and your dealer to live—I choose you. There's still hope for you. You're an idiot but at least you're not some Mexican out there corrupting little kids at the playground."

"My dealer's actually a white guy," the kid said, sweating and squirming under the car tire.

"Eh come on, suck it up, this thing's barely a go-cart, it's not that bad under there," Caesar said, adding, "And believe me, by nature of his vocation itself, your dealer is a Mexican as far as I'm concerned. Bringing that shit into our great country to bring us all down."

"I'm sorry," the kid said, looking up at him wide eyed.

"Damn right you are. Give your dealer a message for me," Caesar said.

He got back in the little car and rolled over the kid's body.

"Tell him to stay the hell away from MY kid!" he shouted out the window.

Then he sped back into the darkness with the guy's yells of pains splitting the silence behind him.

When he got back to the motel room he tossed the keys to the hatchback back onto the table. He went to the sink and scrubbed his hands up to the elbows.

"Honey I'm home. Long day at the office but I think we made real progress today."

As he started to remake his bed, Leo rolled over in the other bed and yawned.

"And what was the point of all this?"

"Isn't it obvious?"

Leo shook his head.

"It proves that I'm a good father. I rehabilitated another bad role model that could later corrupt our boy. That kid was so screwed up he could make a turtle think it's a hare," Caesar said.

He got in bed and pulled the sheet up to his chin.

"Plus I like the car. I don't think it even runs on gas. Fart into the gas tank, lean on the damn thing and you're clear to Maine."

He sighed and closed his eyes, starting to drift off.

"You never said you were sorry for turning on me Leo. If you were sorry, you would have found a way to live."

Silence.

He opened his eyes, looked over at the empty bed next to him and rolled over to face the wall.

When he slept again, he dreamt that he was walking up to a house in the woods, circling it until he finally arrived at a window. He looked down and saw that he was trampling some thick brush. When he looked up again, he was devastated by what he saw through the window.

CHAPTER ELEVEN

BONNIE MEET CLYDE

Caesar strolled into the motel lobby the next morning, bag in hand, wearing "I heart Arizona" sweatpants and a fresh t-shirt with a picture of a skeleton draped over a rock. The skeleton's hand was outstretched and it said, "It's a dry heat."

"Good morning!" he exclaimed cheerfully to the tall old black man, sliding his key across the counter.

"How'd you sleep, friend?" the man asked.

"Best sleep in years, thanks again for your hospitality kind sir," Caesar said.

When the clerk started to print off a receipt from his computer, Caesar slid a twenty-dollar bill across the counter and made eye contact with him. The man pocketed the money, continued printing the receipt, ripped it up and deleted the transaction on the computer screen.

"No problem friend. We specialize in invisible guests," he said smiling.

As Caesar left the lobby, he looked out in the parking lot and froze in his tracks. It was his red Camaro, parked sideways across several spaces. He noticed all new dents and scratches all over the side and silently cursed Tonya for not taking better care of it.

She was standing by the lobby door, gripping the car keys tightly in her fist, examining a small broken rack of tourist brochures circa 1974. Caesar walked over and she looked up. The two locked gazes and Caesar grunted an incoherent greeting.

"Same to you," she said under her breath, pursing her lips together and exposing premature frown lines around her mouth.

He pushed by her out the door into the parking lot. He touched the Camaro's hood gently as he walked by, and then continued on toward the little hatchback.

As he got in the car, a ruckus from inside the lobby wafted outside and caught Caesar's attention. He looked back and saw through the lobby door, the motel front desk clerk wagging a finger and yelling at Tonya.

"Better go check it out and make sure she's OK," Leo advised from the backseat of the hatchback.

"She can take care of herself," he said.

"You know that's not true," Leo said.

He started the car and slowly pulled in front of the lobby door, peering in. The clerk lunged across the counter and grabbed Tonya by the wrist.

"Fire! Fire!" she screeched at the top of her lungs.

Caesar reached in the souvenir bag and fished around for the knife but all he came up with was the empty .45.

"Ah shit," he said, but exited the car, shoving the handgun into his waistband and running inside.

"Hey buddy, what gives?" he demanded of the old man.

"I went out back for one minute, I come out, and she's broken the lock off and got her hand in the cash drawer pocketing bills. I have a good mind to call the cops on her," the clerk said, looking at Caesar, "but I think I'll just handle the situation internally instead."

Caesar was conflicted. Once again, he was presented with clear evidence that Tonya was one of the worst kinds of people on his list—a common thief (unless both her robberies he'd seen were to benefit some sick old relative somewhere). But at the same time he admired her skill. Only one minute to crack open a locked cash drawer? She was pretty talented, especially for someone so young.

"I don't mean to butt in, friend, but what are you planning on doing with her?" Caesar asked the man.

"Are you out of your mind? You're not going to LET him do anything with me, right?" Tonya yelled at Caesar wrenching her wrist free from the clerk's hand in one swift motion.

Caesar looked back and forth between the two. The clerk shrugged. Tonya shot him some fire.

"OK OK," Caesar said, putting his palms in the air in surrender.

"You," he said to Tonya, "how much did you take?"

She hesitated.

"Twenty bucks."

Con to con, he knew she was lying. So did the clerk.

"She's full of shit, I had over two hundred bucks in here, all that's left is a few singles," he protested.

"I know, I know," Caesar agreed.

He turned back to Tonya.

"You're caught red-handed. What's the point?"

"The point is," she said, "that this was a setup. For your information I didn't even have to pick the lock, the cash drawer was wide open. This guy's some kind of narc or something, trying to set up a desperate young girl. What kind of person does that? What's he trying to pull here?"

"She's lying," the man simply said.

"Is she?" Caesar said, scratching his chin. "I wonder… because let's just say she's right and you did have a reason to find a sucker to set up. Who knows how things work in a little nothing of a fucking shithole town in the middle of nowhere? Maybe you had a deal with the local sheriff to bring him a bounty from time to time to prove that crime exists even in little towns; justify his job you know?"

The old black man stood watching him, the corner of his mouth curling up in amusement.

"Or maybe you're part of some underground sex trade and our girl here is a perfect recruit. Maybe you're some liberal heart politico and being part of an underground tunnel that ships little white girls back and forth is your sentimental way of payback for your people."

"Did you just call me a goddamn liberal?" the man demanded.

"I didn't call you shit," Caesar said, "I merely just made some suggestions as to why you'd want to take advantage of an innocent, young girl like this."

Outside, a family in an SUV pulled up and dad, in his Disney t-shirt and ball cap from his favorite team attempted to enter the lobby. Tonya moved like a bolt of lightning to the door, planting a hand on each of his shoulders and pushing him out the door.

"We're closed!" she yelled.

The surprised dad hustled back to his car and Tonya slid the brochure rack in front of the door. The clerk watched with raised eyebrows. Caesar took advantage of the distraction to pull the empty .45 from his waistband and when the clerk looked back, he was looking into the barrel of the gun. He took a quick step to the right out of the line of fire and made a grab for the gun. Tonya gasped.

"Easy man," Caesar warned.

"What're you going to do, take the singles your girlfriend left?" he asked Caesar.

"I'm not robbing you man, I'm..." he looked at Tonya as she returned to his side, "I'm defending the lady's honor."

"Oh is that a fact?" the man asked.

"Yeah it is. We're not leaving until you apologize for setting her up," Caesar said.

"Yeah!" Tonya piped in.

Caesar put his finger to his lips to silence her.

"Do I get my money back if I do?" the clerk asked.

"What do you think?" Caesar asked.

"I think you just implied that the girl stole from me because—what was it again? I set her up? Now if you make the decision to let her steal from me—knowingly and outside of any set up—it's just stealing. Wouldn't you agree?" the clerk said.

Caesar thought about it.

"You know you're right," he said and turned to Tonya. "Give the man his money back. It was wrong for you to take it."

"Are you kidding me?" Tonya cried out.

"I am not. Give it back," Caesar said firmly.

"This is fucking bullshit," Tonya said under her breath, reaching deep into her tight jeans, withdrawing the wad of cash and shoving it across the counter to the clerk.

Caesar caught a slight whiff of the pungent smell attached to the bills from their hiding place. The clerk looked at the pile of money on the counter in front of him, and then back up at Caesar, who was still aiming the gun at him.

Caesar couldn't help himself. He knew it was a stupid move but he looked away for just a split second at Tonya's crotch. And he knew he deserved it when he felt the old man knock the gun out of his outstretched arm onto the floor while simultaneously delivering a vicious blow to the side of Caesar's head with his fist.

Caesar swayed and fell to his knees, gasping for air. He thought he heard Tonya scream but it could have been the shrill ring in his affected ear. He vaguely remembered that there was a gun involved and crawled on his hands and knees around the counter. His father's dog tags slipped out of his collar and hung down as he crawled. Through a blurred veil over his eyes he saw Tonya trying to wrestle the gun away from the clerk. He was about to tell her to be careful when he suddenly remembered the gun was empty. The last clerk he had to deal with had emptied it firing at the sound of a shattering jelly jar.

The old man came up with the gun, holding it in the air out of Tonya's reach, examining it. He started to laugh.

"Well, why am I surprised?" he said, ejecting the empty magazine onto the floor, and pulling the cartridge back to reveal the empty chamber.

Caesar reached for the gun and the clerk gave it back to him.

"I happen to be between ammo," he said, putting the empty gun back into his waistband.

"Seems so," the clerk said.

He pointed at Caesar's neck.

"Whose tags? Assuming not yours since you're still standing here. That'd be like walking around carrying your own grave marker," the old man said.

"They're my father's," Caesar answered.

Tonya got up and leaned on the counter, listening with curiosity.

"Those don't look like the tags of a man killed at war. They're too clean," the man said.

"That's right. Our country dropped him in the jungle to die but he gave 'em the finger and got out anyway," Caesar said proudly.

"And then what?" the man said with a knowing smile.

"Then he came home and spent the rest of his life dealing with bullshit," Caesar responded.

The clerk nodded as if he understood.

"Have you ever heard the term REMF?" he asked Caesar.

Caesar shook his head.

"It stands for rear echelon mother fucker. It's GI slang for a grunt who never did anything. That's what they called me in Korea. And like your dad, I've been back here dealing with bullshit ever since," the clerk said, looking at Tonya.

She looked down, studying the blisters on her fingertips.

"Son, do you know why guys have so much trouble after wars? I don't care if it's one of the great ones, Korea, Vietnam, or one of the recent ones against the cave dwellers. They say war is hell but it's coming home from war that's really hell. And it's not because of what guys did, it's because of what they didn't do."

Caesar absorbed this, slipping into a mental slide show of images of a lost man trying to survive in a world where he didn't belong. He now saw how badly his father tried—to be a good dad, a patient, loving husband, and decent citizen—all while treading in mental molasses, trying to keep his head above the surface and keep breathing. He was trained to be a killer, and then chained to a tree in the backyard until he finally found a way to euthanize himself. Caesar felt a wave of emotion come up in his throat and swallowed hard, looking away from the old man.

"Tell you what," the clerk said, turning his back on Caesar and opening the safe against the wall. "Now I'm gonna do something I probably shouldn't."

Caesar looked at the pile of money on the counter and then over at Tonya. She didn't move a muscle toward it and he nodded at her approvingly.

The old man turned and slapped a box of .45 caliber ammo on the counter.

"Use it wisely," he told Caesar.

Caesar picked up the box. It was full.

"I don't know what to say," he said.

"No words needed. Just keep this young lady here out of trouble. You and I know there's enough trouble out there already. Maybe the world still has a chance though, if we can get to the next generation," the old man said.

Caesar nodded.

"Thank you sir," Caesar said.

The man nodded.

"Come on," he said to Tonya and she followed him out the door.

Behind them the clerk finally picked up the money and returned it to the cash box.

On their way out, Caesar spotted Tonya's guitar case and rucksack near the door, scooped them up and handed them to her.

"Here," he said.

Tonya took them from him, turned and took off across the parking lot past the hatchback, back toward the Camaro. He followed her.

"Stop following me, you're bad luck," she said, turning to wait for him to catch up.

They walked silently to the beaten-up car. When Tonya opened her fist for the keys, Caesar reached over and grabbed them, pushing her out of the way and climbing into the driver's seat.

"Hey!" she protested.

He leaned over and opened the passenger side.

"Get in," he said.

She stood pouting outside his window.

"Oh come on," he urged. "Unless you'd rather take your chances on the eco-mobile over there?"

He handed her the keys to the hatchback.

"I never needed other people's wheels before you made me into a thief and I don't need them again," she huffed.

"I MADE you.... I'm not GIVING you wheels you stu-... You dingbat, I'm offering you a ride, just like you did for me before," Caesar said irritably.

Tonya stood, thinking, and studying him.

"In or out?" Caesar demanded.

She started walking away.

"Oh come on, we're practically Bonnie and Clyde now!" he called out playfully.

The truth was he knew they needed to get the hell out of there. The kindly old hotel clerk was the type who could switch loyalties and turn them over to the local law in a heartbeat.

Tonya turned and looked back at the little hatchback and then at the Camaro, tossing a coy little smile at him before stopping and opening the passenger's side door, depositing her sack and guitar into the backseat.

"So what is it you really want? Are you stalking me or something?" she asked as Caesar exited the motel parking lot and hit the road again.

"Well, I haven't decided yet. But I've noticed you and I seem to be useful to each other so I figure why fix what's broken," he said.

"Funny you say that since the story of my life so far has more to do with being useless and broken," she said, suddenly sounding very grown up.

He looked over at her and for the first time, saw the depth of the movie playing right below the surface.

As they continued driving east, Caesar looked in the rearview mirror. Leo grinned back at him, and then turned around and made himself comfortable in the backseat, sitting cross-legged and looking out the back window at the road behind them.

Caesar and Tonya sped through the desert. He could tell she was nervous, fidgeting with the air controls in the console, back and forth, cold to colder and then back again. He was doing the same with the radio controls.

"Hey I was wondering, why'd you yell fire back there at the motel? If you wanted to get attention wouldn't you yell rape?" he asked.

It was his version of the small talk couples use to diffuse tension on a first date. Tonya stopped fiddling long enough to answer him.

"My mom taught me that when I was little. She was a waitress in a truck stop diner, worked the night shift so she'd have to walk to her car alone at night. She found out the hard way that if you yell rape, people think you're messing around. Like a drunk couple having a fight or even just playing around and stuff, especially the dumb cheerleader types who think that kind of thing is romantic as hell. Yell fire though and people think it might involve them. So they look."

Caesar thought of the sheep at the travel plaza staring at the cracks in the pavement as he kidnapped Marty in plain sight.

"Makes sense. It's fucked up though, the whores who think acts of sexual deviance are a joke," he said.

That earned him a little smile. But then Tonya bit her lip nervously, her eyes sweeping back and forth across the road ahead of them.

"Look, I promise to drop you off if a better offer comes along," he said.

"No offense though," she laughed.

"Of course not. Although you haven't been completely fair to me either," he said, patting the Camaro's dashboard.

"You haven't been paying attention at all if you think that I care about being fair," she responded.

"Quite right, Bonnie. Point taken."

She finally looked at him.

"Sounds like we both got equal hands of fair dealt to us," said Caesar.

"So you're a good bandit then? Like a bloodier Robin Hood?"

"Have I raised a hand to you? Disrespected you in any way?" he asked.

"No," she admitted.

"Then stop acting like you know the reasons behind what I've done. We all work from different codes and you're no different," he said.

She nodded silently and stared out the window.

Caesar stared steadfastly down the road at the horizon. If a guy had challenged him like Tonya did, he'd be rotting in the sun with Marty. But something about the way she talked to Caesar, showed him she wasn't trying to hurt, judge, or make him less of a man (like his mother had tried to do to his father). She was seeing things for what they were. He had a feeling that's how she had survived her life this long. But that still didn't mean he was ready to admit any of this to her.

"So where were you headed… before all this?" he asked.

She shrugged.

"Come on and tell me," he persuaded.

"I seriously don't know. I was thinking… somewhere happy."

"What, like Florida?" he quipped.

"That's a myth!" she exclaimed. "Only about two percent of people there are actually happy. One percent are tourists who get to go home when reality sets in, the others are old people living in air conditioned boxes waiting to die."

"OK, OK… Then what does happy mean to you?" he asked.

"What does it mean to you?" she volleyed back.

"Being with my kid. Being a good dad. Fulfilling my purpose," Caesar said.

"Oh. At least you know," she said distantly, staring out the window.

For a moment, Caesar considered asking her to be the godmother. But when he looked in the rearview mirror to check with Leo, he saw that the backseat was empty. He decided to hold off on popping the question until Leo reappeared so his buddy could have his say in the decision. Besides, he still didn't know this chick well enough to bestow that kind of privilege on her.

Caesar watched the last of the sunset in the rearview mirror, looking for any ominous flashing lights coming over the horizon. They were talking up a storm while looking for a place to stay for the night. As he rambled on, he glanced toward the backseat, thinking of the last person who knew this much about him.

"So of course after that kind of holy hell of a childhood, you'd want to start a family," Tonya said.

"How can you still not get it? I have to be the father that my old man desperately wanted to be, but never could because of the war and then marrying a whore. The most important job a man can have is being a father."

"And for a woman, a mother."

"What?" Caesar was taken off guard.

"The most important job of being a mother," Tonya said with that same faraway, glazed-over stare Caesar was becoming more and more curious about with each passing hour.

"Spoken like a woman," he said, carefully covering his curiosity with sarcasm.

"And, what is it you think I am?"

Caesar looked at her.

"I'd prefer to forget."

"What is it with you and women? You won't screw us, like any other self-respecting woman hater, yet I'm somehow intriguing enough to share your air."

"Nobody said you're intriguing. I'm just doing a helpless woman—a very YOUNG woman—a favor."

"The same helpless woman who has survived on the road this whole time just like you? The same female who you called a thief and helped you get out of that store alive?" she asked.

"The kiss ass in the convenience store was nothing more than a termite. A coward," Caesar responded.

"So I can only deal with cowards? Like my mom's boyfriends and him?"

"By gosh Leo I think she's got it!" Caesar slapped the steering wheel.

"Pull the car over now. I didn't ask to be messed with like this," she said, her hand on the door handle.

"No, but you did tag along, just looking for trouble. Didn't you?"

"You sick son of a bitch. I thought we..."

"Were bonding? Come on sweetheart. I've spent the better part of my life with a dimwitted farm boy who worshipped the ground I walked on. I'm used to having a partner, not a smart ass security risk who could change her mind at any minute and turn me in," Caesar said.

"So you're holding me hostage," she said.

"Hostage? Who should I contact for the ransom money? No, I'm not holding you hostage. I just need some company to make me stand out less," said Caesar.

"And if I leave?"

"You won't. You need me as much as I need you."

"What if a better offer comes along?" she asked, her hand still on the door handle.

Caesar reached over for Tonya's thigh but touched her hand lightly at the last minute before withdrawing back to his side of the car.

"It won't," Caesar said.

Caesar and Tonya sipped coffee in a diner next to their motel, keeping their voices low.

"How much further to Loretta's place?" Tonya asked.

Caesar heard the strain in her voice. She sounded like she had aged ten years since he had first met her.

"I think based on her last letter we'll get there tomorrow night," he said, trying to sound kind but hearing the strain in his own voice too.

"And then what?" she asked.

Caesar sighed into his cold coffee and watched the brown water ripple against the cracked, off-white walls of the mug. He hadn't expected it to be this hard. He knew that leaving the security of prison and then the journey east would be tiresome, but the death of Leo had nuked his spirit. And now being responsible for this girl, and truthfully being attracted to her, was creating a hurdle that he felt almost too exhausted to cross.

"I'll let you know then," he finally answered.

Then he watched Tonya stare at a family making their way out of the diner. She slid a little closer to the aisle. Caesar reached over and patted her hand reassuringly.

"I can't think of a single reason to hurt you Tonya."

"How many reasons have you ever needed?" she asked.

But at least she stopped sliding down the booth toward the aisle.

"Usually just one. But it's almost always the same," he said.

"Do I even want to know?" she frowned; creating even more lines on her face that weren't there before.

"When there's just no reason for the person to exist," Caesar said simply.

"What's my reason then?"

"I already told you," he said.

"I mean after that… after you reunite with your son and his…" she stammered.

"What are you…" he began.

"Nothing. Forget it," she said.

Tears welled up in Tonya's eyes. Caesar squeezed her hand more tightly as he looked in her beautiful eyes and saw his feelings for her reflected back.

"You've been fooling everyone. You're not a little girl at all are you?" he asked.

"What, do you want, ID?" she joked.

The waitress brought the check and Caesar left some of Marty's money on the table.

"Come on," he said, standing and holding out his hand.

She smiled and took it. He led Tonya out of the diner. Any thoughts she had of leaving seemed to disappear as she held onto Caesar's hand for dear life and they made their way through the diner.

Back in the motel room a little later, Tonya lay curled up on the big bed, sobbing. Caesar awkwardly stroked her back, acting the part of a good parent as much as he could distantly remember.

"Shh... Shhh Bonnie," he murmured.

"Tonya!" she cried out and then blew her nose.

"OK... So what do you want from me? You know I can't... well... it wouldn't be... if your purpose is already..." he said, grasping.

"Oh enough with this code, morals, values, purpose, and mission bullshit! You sound like a book. Shut up and talk like a real person for once!" she said.

"I can't kill you if you already want to die! Why won't you believe me?" he said.

"Oh cut the crap, you can't kill anyone anymore! Death is not a purpose! God, you are so screwed up, Caesar!" she yelled leaping to her feet and pacing the room.

He sat on the bed watching her.

"What do you mean I can't kill anymore? I need to clear a path for my kid and unless you have a better idea..."

"If this is the kind of self-righteous shit you plan on raising your son with then you're no better than your mother!" she said, standing over him and jabbing her finger in his face.

He reached up and grabbed her hand so tightly that the ends of her fingers went blue. Rather than wincing, her eyes flashed even more brightly.

"Now you can kill me, right? I just told you what a horrible waste of a father you're going to be. You have no purpose! You're nothing to anyone!"

Caesar let go of Tonya's hand, jumped off the bed with a roar and beat the hell out of it, but didn't lay a finger on Tonya. She did her best to continue leaping in front of him, challenging him, as he purposefully dodged her.

"Come on Caesar! Hit me! I know you want to! You have to! What's the matter with you? Are you a coward?" she yelled.

Caesar bellowed again and attacked the room with vengeance.

"Hey termite! Come on termite! I'm right here! Coward! All you big men are nothing but cowards!" Tonya continued.

They both took out their respective years of pent up rage out on the room in a bizarre dance, until finally they collapsed back onto the bed sweating, tear stained, chests heaving up and down, staring at the ceiling. It took them several minutes to catch their breath and find words.

"I hate that I met you," said Caesar.

"I hate that I met you too," replied Tonya.

Caesar found the energy to prop himself up on one elbow and leaned over Tonya. She reached up to touch his rough, unshaven face. He used his fingers to untangle the knots in her hair. She smiled encouragingly, guiding his face to hers, his lips onto hers and kissing him. The two made love as virgins, everything new and strange and exciting. Age differences, blood-stained clothes (and the reasons for those stains) and their past sins, likely speeding down the highway to catch up with them, disappeared in a tangle of limbs, pasts, emotions, pain, needs and mutual comfort. When they were done, Caesar scooped Tonya into his arms like a child, trying to wrap his mind around what had just happened. Tonya kissed his dirty, scraped up fingers.

"You know I was lying before. I was trying to make you leave so it won't hurt so much when you finally do. I think you'll make a great father," she said.

Caesar kissed her again.

"I'm not going anywhere. You've made that impossible. I don't know what just happened but suddenly I can't imagine being without you," he told her, and he meant it.

"Prove it," she said

He only knew of one way.

"How'd you like to be my son's godmother?" he asked her.

Tonya laughed.

"It would be the greatest honor of my life so far," she said sincerely.

Caesar couldn't stop kissing her. Every time he tried to stop she'd look up at him with those angel eyes of hers and he'd start all over again in a new spot on her body.

The theme song from *Gilligan's Island* woke him up later that night after he and Tonya had finished making love for the third time. At first he thought it was her, restlessly awake, but then he felt her soft, warm body nestled against him and heard her snoring as softly as a kitten. It was Leo who was sitting at the foot of the bed in front of the TV set; once again feeling obligated to make his presence known.

Leo was watching a black and white rerun of the show. Caesar laughed because of all the times he had walked in on his buddy in the common room just like this, cross-legged and thoroughly enjoying the corny comedy with his chin bouncing up and down on his hands every time he laughed. That's exactly what he was doing now, chuck-ling along with the show's tin can laugh track. Caesar crawled down the bed and sat next to him. It was on the tip of his tongue to ask the question he'd wanted to ask all day: "Why Leo, like a persistent ghost of capers past, are you still here?"

"Remember this one Caesar? It's the one where they find the headhunters living on the other side of the island," said Leo, his eyes glued to the exploits of the mislaid charter members of the three-hour tour.

"Yeah, vaguely," said Caesar, staring in wonderment at Leo, fully expecting him to evaporate at any moment.

"See? It's like the headhunters are collecting the souls of their victims. That's why they kill them," said Leo.

"What are you talking about? That's not the point of the epi-sode at all," argued Caesar, gesturing at Gilligan as he scampered in fast motion out of the headhunters' flimsy bamboo cage.

"Maybe, who knows really?"

Leo turned to face Caesar and he noticed an eerie yellow glow in his dead partner's eyes.

"People like them, who live in the middle of nowhere for all that time, waiting for visitors to come along to feed on… that the headhunters might also be taking people's sins and souls when they shrink their heads," he said.

Pissed off at nearly falling for his expired buddy's obvious ploy, Caesar jumped up and started pacing around.

"I don't recall the ghost of Christmas future using crappy sit-coms to make his point. Is this the best you can do?" he demanded.

Leo was unfazed, staying cross-legged on the bed and following Caesar around the room with his hollow backlit gaze.

"Have you really thought about what happens to the souls of the people you kill?" he asked.

"They die," replied Caesar. "And they bring all the nastiness and bad influence that my kid would have been exposed to, straight to hell with them."

"And you don't think any of it gets on you on the way out?" Leo asked.

"It's not like changing motor oil, Leo."

"How do you know?"

"Stop asking me that. I know what I know and you've got no right to keep bugging me. Not anymore," said Caesar.

When he looked up again Leo was sitting in a chair by the door.

"Is this the plan? Keep torturing me for the rest of my life with the same bullshit questions you hounded me with when you weren't a stupid ghost?" demanded Caesar.

"Maybe," shrugged Leo.

"You are such a…"

Before Caesar could finish his irate sentence, he awoke in the darkened motel room with Tonya meshed into his body. He still heard Leo's voice in his head though.

"What you think is being cleansed, is really being cemented."

Caesar's eyes darted around in the dark before closing again.

"I tell you buddy," he whispered, "even if I believed you, I wouldn't even know where to start fixing it."

CHAPTER TWELVE
BROKEN ANGEL

Caesar peed into the rusty toilet bowl, wincing because of his oversexed night with Tonya, but nevertheless contented. Tonya entered the motel bathroom with her toothbrush and toothpaste, craned her neck around, and kissed him as he continued peeing.

"Good morning," she said sweetly and began brushing her teeth.

"Hey... Um, is this normal?" he asked.

"Mmm... Sure, why not?" she responded through the toothpaste in her mouth.

Caesar finished peeing and found a corner of the sink to stand in front of as he gave himself a much-needed shave. Tonya finished brushing and took her turn on the toilet. Caesar looked down at her, but figuring this too was normal, carried on with his shaving.

"So, I was wondering about something," he said.

"Oh yeah, what?"

She finished on the toilet and squeezed back into the counter space to wash her hands. Caesar moved back into the room.

"What's with the guitar? Do you really play or are you packing heat?" he called out.

"What do you think?" she giggled, coming out of the bathroom and plopping down on the bed with the remote.

"I don't know. I've never known any musicians... or anybody with any kind of talent. I wasn't sure..." said Caesar.

He laid the guitar case on the bed in front of her. She looked at it for a second, and then returned to flipping through television channels.

"Would you look at this, another one of those sleeping pill commercials," Tonya said. "You might end up waking up in the middle of the night, fly into a fit of rage, beat the crap out of your kids, not remember a thing and then contemplate suicide over your latte the next day, but hey, sweet dreams."

"Stop trying to change the subject, do you play or not?" Caesar asked her.

"Um yeah. I really play. I haven't since I left. But seeing it was the only thing that made my life bearable I thought I should keep it. Just in case," she said, settling on a cartoon.

"So you only play if life is unbearable?"

"So far," she answered him.

"Could you make an exception?"

Tonya blushed but kept her eyes on the television set.

"You really want me to?" she asked, fingering the latch on the case thoughtfully.

"Yeah," he said, hitting the power button on the TV remote control, "I do."

Tonya glanced at him and then got up shyly, grabbed her guitar from the corner, took it out of its case, dusted it off and sat on the edge of the bed. She thought of the last time she'd played, Christmas songs at the shelter. How far away California seemed right now that she was deep in the desert on a rescue mission with a man she barely knew, yet felt like she'd known in a different lifetime.

She tuned the guitar, her fingers caressing each individual string until the tones united into one melodic chord. When Tonya finally looked up, she saw that she had Caesar's complete attention. Nobody had ever looked at her with such complete focus. Tonya felt naked for the first time in front of him.

"I don't know what to play."

"Yes you do."

"But it's been so long," she protested.

Caesar simply smiled at her, until she finally began to sing.

"You think you're where you wanna be... You've finally settled down... You're sure the world you've figured out... Will hold when chips are down... What you hadn't counted on... A view of your own box... You're nothing but a prisoner... It's you who turned the lock... Your will has never been your own... To others you concede... You think that you're not worth enough... To do much more than breathe... It's time to take a stand my friend... Take back the life that's yours... Today you'll risk it all to find... The key on Canyon Road... You've got to be free... A mind of your own... You've got to be free...

All out on your own... You've got to be free... The earth is yours to roam...

You've got to be free... 'Cuz it's a long road home."

When she finished and finally looked at him, Caesar was looking away across the room. Leo was back. He was sitting at the table across the room, tears rolling down his face. Caesar couldn't figure out what was making him cry. It was just a stupid song.

"Oh my God. Are you OK?" Tonya put the guitar down and scrambled up the bed, looking at him with concern.

"What do you mean?" he asked her.

Caesar realized that the tears were streaming down his own face. Embarrassed, he reached up and wiped them away. Tonya snuggled up to him and grasped his hand. He tried to push her away but she wouldn't let go.

"No, no. It's nothing... I'm just... You know I just never realized..." he stammered.

There weren't enough guns and cops in the world to make his heart pound as fast as it was now. She was a part of him now.

"I didn't realize either, until I decided to trust you instead of kicking your ass," she said seriously.

"First of all, there's no way. And second of all, that's what it took to free you?" he asked.

"From myself, yeah. Trusting someone is something I've never done before. What about you?"

"I don't know yet," he admitted.

"You will."

"How?" he asked.

He didn't really want to know the answer. His head hurt from the responsibility of the conversation.

"If I figured it out, so can you," she said and kissed him.

"By the way, where's this Canyon Road place, like in the song?" he asked.

"You know, it's weird," Tonya admitted. "I dreamt about this street sign one night that said that. It was in the woods."

Caesar nodded, remembering his dream.

Caesar and Tonya were closing in on Loretta and the kid (or baby; the math had become fuzzy in his mind). This had been the most exciting part of the journey so far for both of them and in a strange way they were glad to share it with each other.

A few hours after (eventually) leaving the motel, as they headed north, Tonya was the first to point out the transition in scenery from brown to green. She carefully read out loud the directions they got from a local store clerk, to Loretta's last known residence. From there it was a door-to-door scavenger hunt. Each house, apartment and trailer was tucked deeper into the sea of green. Each occupant scribbled yet another forwarding address on a piece of paper for Caesar and Tonya. But instead of getting closer, Caesar felt like he was drifting further and further away from his family reunion.

The two were walking through a trailer park as Caesar pulled out a rumpled, stained letter in an envelope postmarked several times with several prison review and approval stamps. Tonya stood on her tiptoes, trying to get a peek at it.

"This was the original letter telling me I had a son," Caesar said, answering her silent question.

"A good day?" she asked.

"The best day of my life."

She kissed him for the first time that morning. Caesar was still intrigued and slightly confused by all of this, but played along, trying to act like a man would in this situation. He also realized he had gotten used to the comfort of her company. As he unfolded the letter, the belly photo slid out and floated to the ground. Tonya picked it up and held it next to Caesar's face.

"Nice looking family," she said.

"Yes, we will be."

Tonya suddenly realized how close the end of her fantasy was. After being held prisoner in a hell called Shady Acres, she had finally flown free, only to be toyed with in this man—this criminal's—fantasy world. She wondered what she was supposed to do once Caesar stepped into this new reality as husband and father. It was unfortunate that only Caesar could see Leo. Tonya could have used a friend like that now. The belly photo slid from her hands but she caught it before it touched the ground and shoved it back into Caesar's hands.

"What's the address?" she asked.

"Number 14A Redwood Lane," Caesar read from the last slip of paper they'd received.

He looked around at the confusing clumps of street signs and trailers that didn't appear to be attached to any of them.

"How do we..." he started

Pleased to remain distracted, Tonya grabbed the paper from Caesar and took the lead.

"You're on my turf now," she said confidently.

Caesar fell in step behind her as she wove through the trailers, up and down winding dirt roads. She paused in front of a building with "Rec Room" stenciled on the window.

"Hey we had one of these," Caesar said.

Tonya didn't hear him, lost in her thoughts. She pressed her face against the door, remembering the hours, days, and years of her childhood in the Shady Acres rec room that she'd never get back. She suddenly saw a flickering flame, and jumped back before realizing it was someone inside lighting a cigarette.

A nicely dressed woman in a sweater and plaid skirt came over to the door with a big warm smile. Tonya saw a group of people sitting in a circle of plastic folding chairs. The woman opened the door.

"Are you here to join us?" she asked, still smiling.

"To do what?" Tonya asked.

The woman pointed to a cardboard sign on an easel: "Alcoholics Anonymous—Unity, Service, Recovery."

Caesar took note of the folding table with Dixie cups, bright red punch, and chocolate chip cookies.

He began to laugh and Tonya elbowed him.

"No thank you, ma'am," Tonya said politely and tried to steer Caesar away from the door.

He slipped right around her to the refreshment table and helped himself. Tonya stood in the doorway, folded her arms and rolled her eyes. He smiled playfully at her before approaching the group.

"Is there something you'd like to share?" the smiling woman asked.

Standing at the edge of the circle, Caesar looked at her expectantly.

"This is where you're supposed to introduce yourself," an over-weight man in a bulging Jerry Garcia t-shirt said testily, folding his arms and glaring at the intrusion.

"Ah," Caesar said and grabbed a folding chair that was propped against a wall and squeezed into the circle.

"I remember how this works from when I tagged along with my dad as a kid," he explained. "He tried this, well, more than a few times. Can't say that it ever took though."

He thought back to all the sugar highs of his childhood courtesy of gallon after gallon of Hi-C fruit punch and pound after pound of Nestle Toll House chocolate chip cookies.

"You gonna eventually tell us who in the hell you are?" the fat man yelled.

"Jimmy, enough!" the lady in charge told him firmly.

"Nope he's right, I didn't follow the rules. My apologies sir, lady, everyone, hello, my name is Leo and I..." Caesar stopped and looked behind him at Tonya, still holding up the doorframe. He winked at her.

"And I believe that you all believe this is working," he said, folding his arms over his chest and leaning back in his folding chair with a shit-eating grin.

Jimmy's seatmates had to pull the fat man back into his chair.

"OK, OK everyone calm down, let's hear him out," the woman said.

"That's right," Caesar said pointing at the sign on the easel, "that must be what it means by unity. We're all in this together right? You drink, I drink, we all drink! Suck down that pseudo religious self-righteous bullshit by the Kool-Aid gallon and if anyone tries to bring logic or reason into the conversation, start reciting the steps like robots. All for one and one for all right kids? Give me unity or give me death! And in my dad's case, it was the second one!"

"That's not what it means and if you've been to meetings with your dad, you damn well know that!" an indignant mommy type in the corner of the circle said, flushing pink.

"Yeah!" various other members of the group chimed in.

The sweater-skirted leader waved her arms around like a monkey trying to catch a vine, desperately trying to restore order. Her little punch-sipping circle though, was out of order. Caesar quietly got up and started backing away from the circle and the verbal arrows being fired at him. Tonya finally got ahold of him and steered him right out the door but just as she got him out, he pressed his middle finger into the window in the door, right between "rec" and "room."

She continued propelling him down the dirt path and around the corner checking over her shoulder to see if the now incensed mob was following them.

"What the HELL was that all about?" she demanded, her voice rising.

"Revenge," he said.

"What?"

"Why do you care?' he asked.

"I don't," she said, trying to be casual. "I'm just curious what you have against those people."

"Bullshit you don't care. From the moment we got here you've had this attitude like these are somehow your people and you have some special bond with them. I know you grew up in a place like this, but I thought you ended up hating it. You even mentioned wanting to torch the whole fucking place," Caesar said.

Tonya came to a dead halt in the middle of the road and jabbed her index finger into the center of Caesar's chest.

"Let's get something straight, I did NOT burn down Shady Acres! I don't care what you've heard or what you think, that shit was not my fault! That place was ALL I had! Those people were my family!" she yelled.

"Whoa whoa, easy there, I only know what you said, what else could I know? Easy there Bonnie," he said, rubbing her shoulders.

She shook her head clear, took some breaths, nodded and they continued down the road.

"You never answered my question," she reminded him.

"Oh yeah, the unifiers back there," Caesar said sarcastically as they continued walking.

Tonya continued taking note of the street names and numbers on the trailers, checking them against the slip of paper.

"I hate them. I hate them all," he said, adding, "They killed my father."

"Literally?" she asked.

"No Einstein, not literally. But for all the times he showed up, it was like neglect. A man is dying in a ditch on the side of the road, you drive by, slow down and pretend like you're gonna stop but then you keep driving, spraying mud in his face as you pull away. That's what AA did to my dad. They kept saying how they wanted to help him, but then they ended up leaving him there in the ditch with shit all over his face. It might not have been the booze that killed him, but it certainly didn't give him much to live for either," Caesar said.

Tonya nodded respectfully and stayed quiet in reverence for the dead. They walked in silence from there until she finally spotted her target, the main office at the end of the road.

"The office manager. The epicenter of trailer park knowledge, directions and gossip," she announced.

They entered the tiny office. The pseudo couple was soon standing at the office manager's desk, Tonya reading from the slip of paper about Loretta.

"Anything you can tell us about her? We're both really excited to see our—sister—again," she finished.

The manager, a round little man, laughed at the obvious lie and went over to the file cabinet. Flipping through he glanced over at the dust-coated, road-weary couple.

"I haven't had anyone by that name on the property for at least five years," he grumbled.

"That long?" Caesar asked.

"Yeah and if you all are kin, like you said, wouldn't you know that?" the manager asked.

"I've been traveling on the road for work," Caesar said quickly.

Caesar didn't care how his well-rehearsed line would be received until the manager decided to challenge him.

"Oh I'm sure."

"What's that supposed to mean?" Caesar snapped.

"It means I'm so sick of people thinking that I'm some dumb trailer park lackey who doesn't know he's being lied to all the time. Why do you people think you can talk to me like this? So what's it this time? You two look more like con artists than collections people, more like losers than lawyers…"

Caesar lunged over the desk.

"Listen here you son of a bitch!"

Tonya grabbed his elbow, pulling him back before he could make contact with the little man.

"Honey…" she attempted her best impression of a demure little lady, smiling apologetically at the manager.

"Brother and sister my ass," the bald man mumbled.

"Sorry, we've had a long trip," she finished.

"Nobody said anything about being sorry," Caesar said sourly.

"Honey…" Tonya yanked him toward the door while whispering. "Also the epicenter of local off duty law enforcement. Come on."

Caesar stopped at the door and the office manager started dialing.

"One last thing," Caesar said. "Did she leave a forwarding address?"

The office manager glared but opened the file folder again.

Moments later Caesar grinned as they exited the office, reading a piece of paper. Tonya was still fuming as they walked back through the park to the Camaro. Caesar finally noticed.

"What's the matter with you?"

"You almost ruined everything!" she exclaimed and punched him. "Asshole!"

"What are you talking about? I just asked for some information and I got it!" he replied hotly.

They arrived at the car and drove off just as the sun began to set. Caesar studied the paper again as he drove.

"Stop looking at that! Look at me when I'm talking to you," Tonya said, sounding uncharacteristically like a normal nagging broad.

"Listen, dearest, I don't know who you've turned into, but you'd better turn back before I dump your sorry little ass on the side of the road!"

"I knew it! Men never change!"

"Never change?" Caesar laughed. "Did I lay a hand on that misguided little weeble back there? And sure I had that friendly disagreement with those poor, addicted, morally weak people in the common room, but did I try and rehabilitate them in any way? By my scorecard—I'm a changed man!"

"That's how you measure rehabilitation? By how often you're able to restrain yourself from doing bad things?" she asked.

"Who said I thought any of those things were bad? In fact, the reasons I've done things like that is for the GOOD of my son! Why should he grow up around such weakness?"

"So why haven't you touched anyone since the store?" Tonya asked him.

Caesar frowned and drummed his fingers on the steering wheel, choosing not to tell her about the druggie in the nighttime desert.

"Because I love him enough to admit that my way of dealing with this stuff, might not be the best way anymore," Caesar said quietly, looking in the rearview mirror for Leo.

"Pull over," Tonya said quietly.

"What? Why?" Caesar asked.

"Pull over now."

Curious, he did as she asked.

She got out of the car and reached into the back seat for her things, avoiding eye contact with him.

"Tonya, what do you think you're doing?"

When she looked up at him, the sadness on her face made Caesar's stomach clench.

"Do you still have it?" she asked.

"Of course," he said, pulling the belly photo out of his pocket.

Tonya grabbed it from his hands and held it in front of his face.

"You don't need me anymore Caesar. You have everything you need to go home to your family now."

"Tonya!"

As she walked away, Caesar watched the photo flutter down onto the front seat. He stared down at his family. Then he looked up at Tonya again and remembered a conversation they'd had recently.

They were lying in the cool desert sand under the velvet horizon wrapped in the blankets from the nun at the mission.

"I want the story," murmured Tonya, kissing Caesar's neck.

He turned and looked at her. She was curled up like a kitten in his arms. He liked how her hair had grown long. She kept complaining how it was getting harder to manage, constantly tugging it into an unruly ponytail, but he liked it wild. He inhaled the blonde tangled waves draped over his shoulder.

She had been pleading to hear "the story." She wanted to hear the mystical tale that would finally explain this man that she had fallen in love with so completely and unexpectedly, against any shred of rational judgment. She knew how the story ended, here in his arms, still on the run from the convenience store debacle, but deliriously happy just to be with him. Tonya desperately needed to know how the story began. She needed to know how someone she could be so in love with could fall so far off the tracks without realizing it.

"I want the story," she repeated.

"Well, I'll tell you," he sighed, "there's another guy who liked to hang out in the desert who beat me to it. He told a version of my story in one of his songs."

"I think I know that guy. He wrote some songs that gave me something to hope for," Caesar's kitten purred into his chest.

Caesar recited some of the words that mirrored his own life. Tonya murmured some of the lyrics along with him, drumming her fingers on his chest.

"The killer awoke before dawn... he put his boots on... And he walked on down the hall... and he came to a door... and he looked inside... Father, yes son? I want to kill you. Mother? I want to..."

He stopped, pushing all the air from his lungs in an effort to purge the emotions of those words.

"What did you want to do to your mother?" asked Tonya, propping herself up on her elbow and leaning over him so her hair fell onto his face.

"Same thing the lizard king did, I suppose," he said, staring off into space.

He was back in the hallway of his childhood home again, outside his parents' bedroom door, narrating the past from the present.

"What did I want to do? I wanted to make her unborn and me with her. I was insulted by her very existence."

He remembered quietly nudging the door open and watching his mother bob rhythmically up and down to the squeaking of the bedsprings, making love to a man that wasn't his father.

"For as far back as I can remember, she did nothing but shit on my father's dignity and piss on the sacred institution of marriage. She was a whore and for most of my life that's exactly what I thought of women—that they were all good-for-nothing whores."

Caesar glanced over at Tonya to see if she had taken offense to this. She smiled knowingly at him so he didn't have to ask the question.

"That's my mom, not me. And it's not all women either Caesar. But the ones you're talking about, I've known them. I've seen them. I can't say for sure if they really deserve what they get but sometimes it sure seems like it, doesn't it?" said Tonya.

"Maybe," said Caesar, pausing to ponder the idea before continuing his story.

Back in his parents' bedroom he was holding his mother and her lover at gunpoint.

"I was ready to kill her. And I think I would have, if my only living hero hadn't walked in and taken the gun out of my hand," he said, watching in his mind as his father entered the bedroom and unclasped Caesar's teenage fingers from around the gun, taking it away.

"The lover had already fled from me into the bathroom and was hoping to flush himself out of the whole disgusting situation. He didn't get very far though. My father exploded the guy's brains all over my mom's ugly pink Mary Kay makeup collection."

Caesar's heart pounded and he felt sick to his stomach, remembering what it felt like to experience death for the very first time, permeating all of his senses.

When he opened his eyes, he was back lying under the blanket in the desert, staring up at the starry night sky. Tonya was propped up on her elbow gazing down at him, eagerly awaiting the long-awaited story's conclusion.

"And?" she asked breathlessly.

"And, justice was done," said Caesar.

"But I thought you said your mom was more at fault. What happened to her?" Tonya asked.

He saw a brilliant flash of a naked Mary Magdalene with the hand of God coming down and wrapping itself around her neck, choking red screeching demons out the top of her head.

"I don't know. My father told me to leave and never come back," he said, intentionally leaving the part out about what he saw when he did return briefly to the bedroom window.

He returned his attention to the desert and Tonya. She was looking at him in utter adoration.

"What?" he asked her.

"You haven't always been a killer. You were just a scared kid," she said rather triumphantly.

Caesar looked at Tonya as if she'd just revealed who killed Kennedy.

"That's right. I was," he said.

"So the way you turned out isn't totally your fault then," she continued on, taking her best shot at repentance through rationalization and hoping some might rub off on her.

Caesar looked at her adoringly.

"Tonya that doesn't make me innocent either. No matter how fucked up things are, we still get a little bit of free will to play with. Sure I used mine to make the decision to punish evil instead of seeking out good, and I've got to live with that. But if I blame who I am based on being a scared kid, well then, we're nothing but a whole society full of excuses aren't we?"

"I guess," she said, tracing shapes in the dirt with her finger, avoiding his gaze.

"You know," he said, "back when I was locked up I used to fantasize about how everything would have been different if I was a better kid, or even just more normal."

Cue cheerful little Caesar in spotless school clothes, skipping through the front door with a wide, pearly white grin. Mother emerges from the kitchen, also smiling while drying a pot.

"Hello darling how was your day. Did you make any new friends today?"

Father comes in from the garage with a wrench wiping his greasy hands on his overalls.

"Hello son, how was your day? What did you learn today?"

He tousles Caesar's shiny, clean, fine, brown hair that is nothing at all like an out-of-control Brillo pad.

Lying there, losing himself in the starry blanket overhead, and watching the idyllic scene play out in his mind, Caesar felt the weight of intense longing settling into his chest. He squeezed his eyes shut, begging God for a do-over.

"But I get the feeling I was never normal enough for my parents and that was the thing that set everything off balance. Like a teeter-totter. I teetered so they tottered. Then we all fell down."

Tonya nodded.

Then Caesar remembered something.

"Hey, you said I haven't always been a killer. So that's how you see me now?" he asked.

"Do you deny that you have killed?" she asked.

The hairs on Caesar's arms stood up.

"No. But when I have been in the position where I have had no choice but to take a life, it was for the common good. I don't accept being called a killer—not the way you mean it, the way society does," he said.

"Since when do you consider me society?" she asked in a way that disappointed him.

"What's your point?" she asked.

"You got your story. Go to sleep Tonya," Caesar said, turning away from her.

He left Tonya lying awake until a single ray of the rising sun hit her between the eyes. She glanced over at Caesar, checking the security of his gun before carefully placing it in his bag. Pangs of guilt stabbed her when she realized she felt lucky that it was only a ray of sun that hit her between the eyes.

Back in real time, on the side of the highway, Caesar looked up from the photo down the road where Tonya had disappeared. He recalled how hard the newly minted couple had to work in the hours following that incident, to trust each other again. Tonya had to regain Caesar's trust in her identity as the opposite of every woman he'd ever known. Caesar had a much tougher job. He had to convince her that the road of change and redemption that she was leading him down wasn't a desert mirage.

Now, looking at the dark empty road, he realized how much he would miss her—and the thought terrified him.

CHAPTER THIRTEEN
CANYON ROAD

This time Caesar didn't chase her. He spun the car around and sped off in the opposite direction. In the rearview mirror, he took one last look at Tonya as she walked toward the lights of the nearest town, ponytail bobbing in time with the sway of her hips. He thought that it might be this girl, this woman, who would be the death of him, not Leo as he'd always thought. He refocused his eyes in the rearview mirror and saw that the backseat was still empty.

Caesar was elbow deep in the nighttime darkness as he wound his way up the narrow forest roads leading to Loretta's last known address. The car's headlights were the only lights other than the moon, which kept disappearing behind clouds, reminding Caesar of the prison searchlights whenever it reappeared. He automatically checked the rearview mirror for blue flashing lights, while simultaneously believing that the cops were probably long off his trail by now. He knew what it felt like to be chased and he distinctly felt like the chaser, not the target right now.

Winding his way around another sharp embankment of trees, he finally found what he was looking for—the dirt road with a street sign marked "Canyon Road." He would walk the rest of the way on foot. He wanted to surprise Loretta, not alarm her, and certainly not give her time to make any unnecessary phone calls. He needed time to plead his case and make her realize the importance of a father in their son's life. Families needed to stay together and it was his job to make his baby's mother realize that.

Caesar parked the car deep in the trees, reached into the souvenir bag and pulled out the .45 and the box of ammo from the motel clerk, loading it, and shoving it in his back waistband. When he put the box of ammo back in the bag his fingers brushed up against the teddy bear. He took it out, flipped on the interior light and looked at it. The blood had turned into a brown crust, staining half its face.

"Time to meet your godson buddy," Caesar said, grabbing the bear by its arm and flipping off the light.

He set off on foot toward the faint yellow lights in the distance. As he trudged forward, he realized how close he was getting to his dream. Caesar began to breathe faster, finally hyperventilating so much that he lost focus and tripped over a log and crashed to the ground headfirst. He felt a cool sensation against his forehead and squinted in the dark, tracing his fingers over a concrete surface. His fingertips made their way through the engravings of a person's name… and then some dates. Caesar was lying on someone's grave. He almost leapt up but found himself enjoying the smooth, cool surface so he lay there awhile, staring up at the starry sky.

"Been running toward this for years... Leo... There's nothing to be afraid of, right?" he murmured.

"This is your last chance Caesar."

Caesar sat up and peered around in the darkness. He could barely make out Leo's shadow behind a nearby tree. His voice was growing faint. Caesar sat up but made no effort to chase the ghost this time.

"You know buddy, I was thinking about what you were saying before, that I'm absorbing all the sins of my victims to pass on to my kid," he said.

"Sins of the father," Leo said softly.

"How come you were never this poetic when you were alive?" Caesar asked.

The leaves of the thick wall of trees around him rustled softly.

"Well Dickens, I've decided you're full of shit," Caesar said, quickly adding, "Or at least your theory is."

"Really Caesar? Is there a commandment I'm forgetting? Or are you just making up new ones as you go along now to back up your story?" Leo asked.

"Is that it? I'm wrong for striking down sinners to create a better world for my son and other true believers? The same way that God used to in biblical times, before evil won out, took over the world and made it impossible for him to sift through the masses and smite those who need to be—smited. That makes me a bad person?" Caesar raged into the moist darkness.

"You are so very blind Caesar. The only way that God cleansed the world was by sacrificing his only son, to absorb the sins of people like you—like us," Leo said.

"I'm sure we'll settle this eventually Leo. Until then, go find a house to haunt," Caesar said.

He crossed himself, got up, and continued up the road toward the glowing yellow lights. When he emerged from the darkness he stood in the front yard of a well lit home. Assorted children's toys surrounded him. He gripped the teddy bear tightly.

As he continued to the front door, Caesar suddenly remembered his dream and walked around the side of the house instead. He spotted the very same window with the light glowing warmly from within. He was aware of this moment from every angle; every one of his senses was heightened. It was the first time in his life that real life felt exactly like a dream.

Caesar was inches from the window, holding his breath. He looked in, and for a split second, saw his parents' dead bodies sprawled on the retro shag carpeting, his father lying on top of his mother, as if shielding her from his own bullets.

Caesar blinked and remembered to breathe again.

Behind the actual window glass, a toddler sat on an area rug happily playing. The belly had become a baby boy. Caesar smiled, breathing a huge sigh of relief and drinking in the scene he had been dreaming of since the day he received the letter. Overcome with emotion, he pressed his hands flat against the windowpanes.

From inside, Caesar's unshaven, dirty face and grown out straggly hair grew alarmingly large in the window. His son tilted his head up and looked directly at him. In a flash, the boy went from cheerful cherub to terrified toddler, letting out a high-pitched, window-rattling shriek and dropping his toy. Caesar jumped back, staring in horror at what he caused.

A beautiful, well-dressed woman swept in like a mother bird and cradled the boy in her arms. Loretta, the night manager at a Taco Bell when he first met her, was now a polished middle-class housewife. She was nearly unrecognizable to him. Caesar remained motionless, staring at an intimate scene where he clearly did not fit. His eyes started to gloss over and lose focus. His ears filled with the screeching intensity of his son's screams. When his eyes regained focus, Caesar saw Loretta dive for the phone, never taking her eyes off the window. He didn't know whether she was calling because she recognized him or because she did not. This was his last chance.

"No, wait!" Caesar yelled.

He darted around the side of the house to the front door, knocking and calling frantically through the door.

"Please! You don't understand! I'm not here to hurt anyone... I... I..."

Caesar's mind filled with more words than he could clearly process so he abruptly stopped talking. Loretta appeared in a window to the side of the door, phone still in her hand, and baby on her hip. She stopped, as if something struck her as familiar. He couldn't think of anything else to say so he stood staring through the glass at his family.

"My husband will be home any minute," Loretta shouted through the window, trying to wound Caesar.

"Yes, I would guess so. But your husband has nothing to worry about," Caesar yelled back.

Loretta protectively cradled their son.

"What do you want?"

Caesar got close to the window so Loretta could hear him. He saw the green light on her cordless phone still on and knew that someone else was also listening. He didn't care. He was speaking to Loretta, his son, Leo, and Tonya.

"I'm sorry. I believe I just got lost for a while. Sometimes men do that when they won't stop and ask for directions. That's what I like about women. They stop and figure out where they're going... before... Well, God should've added that to his commandments I think. Thou shalt always ask for directions."

Loretta's eyes widened, she dropped the phone and nearly dropped their son.

"To his... Added to his what?" she stammered, white faced.

Caesar saw that she was ready to believe.

"His commandments. Ma'am."

She rushed to open the door, but Caesar grabbed the doorknob quickly to prevent it from turning.

"You don't want to do that," he shouted through the door.

"Why not?" Loretta countered, playing tug of war with the doorknob as their son started a renewed fit of wailing.

Caesar firmly grabbed the doorknob to make her stop turning it. If she opened that door it would be over. His greatest hopes for himself would be realized which he now knew would be a slow death for his family.

"It's best you keep—your son—away from new people... Especially now. When he doesn't know the difference between family and strangers," Caesar said.

The doorknob finally stopped turning and Caesar let go. Loretta moved back to the side window, still cradling their son.

"I have to go now," he told them.

He made himself leave, ferociously holding back tears, nails digging into his hands. Loretta called from inside the window.

"Wait! Please! Caesar!"

He paused, but didn't turn to face her.

"What is it, baby?" he called out.

"He needs his father!" she yelled.

Headlights appeared in the distance.

"He's almost home," Caesar yelled back.

Then, he disappeared into the woods, the lights of the house growing distant as he ran faster and faster away from it. As he ran, he could have sworn that he saw the blurred shapes of his victims stepping out from the darkness of the cemetery into the road—the gas station attendant, the store clerk, the Malibu brat, and finally... Leo.

Caesar woke up and he was still lying on the cool concrete gravestone, staring at the same stars, winking at him to make sure he got the joke. He reached up and felt the egg on his forehead from his fall. In his vision, he had been sweating and out of breath from the sprint away from Loretta's house. His breathing was fine now and he wasn't any sweatier than he was since parting ways with Tonya.

He sat up and peered into the darkness. Not a single warm yellow glow from a house light glowed back at him. He knew he was alone in the woods. What he didn't know was how he would ever get out.

"Caesar, over here," a male voice said.

When Caesar crossed the graveyard, he was only marginally surprised to find Leo sitting cross-legged on another grave.

"Well it's about time you showed up again buddy," Caesar retorted, preparing to lay in on his delinquent friend, thus restoring balance in their friendship.

"Caesar, stop," Leo said wearily.

"You don't get to call the shots Leo, even if you are... well, you know what I mean. Besides, I need your help finding Loretta. I got information that this is the last place she was living but I think he was either messing with me..."

"Caesar, it's time to stop pretending."

The lack of emotion in Leo's voice kept Caesar from talking back for the first time ever. He stood in front of the grave, staring into Leo's eyes instead of the markings on it.

"You remember how you told me before we left jail, about how everything would be easier if we pretended it would be?" Leo asked.

Caesar nodded.

"You said that as long as we knew that WHAT we did wasn't as important as WHY we did it, God would understand and everything would turn out OK. You said that..."

"I know what I said Leo, what's your point?" Caesar said, walking in circles around the graveyard, plotting his next move and trying to ignore Leo.

"It's time to stop pretending Caesar. There's nothing good that can come of it and nobody left to pretend for. Once in awhile you've just got to forget about stuff that you don't need to know about anymore, and carry on with the new stuff you're supposed to be thinking about."

Leo was almost a complete blur. Since he'd never seen a real person go out of focus before, he figured that what Leo was saying must have some truth to it.

"What is it I'm supposed to be forgetting about then?" he challenged, but only half-heartedly.

"Everything you thought you wanted. Everything you thought you've been running away from and running toward at the same time. Caesar, don't you see? You've been running toward that belly for so long that it stopped being real—miles ago," said Leo.

Leo's form was nothing more than a hazy blur of light over the headstone now, but the voice coming from within was crystal clear.

"It's time to see things as they really are, and not how you need them to be," the voice from within the haze said.

"But Leo, I..."

The haze had cleared away and whatever was left of Caesar's memory of Leo had disappeared before his eyes. What remained, however, was the answer to his unanswered question. Caesar saw the names engraved on the headstone in front of him. The grave was overcome with weeds.

The first name had lived for thirty-four years, the second, for just a day. Caesar dropped to his knees and bowed his head. He had not been invited to attend Loretta's funeral nor the one for their child, but in a way he felt like tonight was a special ceremony for just the three of them. It was a birthday, a funeral and a family reunion.

Caesar's tears soaked the dirt in front of the grave. He cried for his childhood, his parents, his life, the lives that he had taken, Leo, and all the other reasons that God refused to trust him with another soul to care for. Kneeling six feet above the family he had been dreaming of for so long now, Caesar felt ready to be reborn. He kissed each name on the headstone, lingering on his son's name.

Caesar felt something in his hand, looked down and realized he was gripping the teddy bear tightly, just like in his vision. He kissed it and placed it on his son's grave.

Then he took off running out of the cemetery, out of the mossy darkness, and back toward the light.

CHAPTER FOURTEEN
GOODBYES

Caesar stumbled out of the woods falling to his knees in the abrasive gravel of the main road, trying to catch his breath.

"Shit!"

Shaking his head, he got up and walked in the direction of the town that he last saw Tonya walk off toward. In the waistband of his pants, the gun dug into his back. He took it out, looked around and spotted a trashcan. Without hesitation Caesar tossed it in with a thud. As he continued walking, cloaked by the darkness, his clothes were now weighing on him. He began stripping off the filthy souvenir clothes he'd been wearing for days, tossing them to the side of the road.

He was standing nude, wearing only his father's dog tags, high atop the gravel road for only a few chilly moments before he saw the bargain motel pool at the bottom of the hill. Only Caesar didn't see a swimming pool, he saw a baptismal pool of water that would take away all his sins and let him start fresh. He had already died and been reborn in the cemetery after all.

He half ran, half slid down the dirt hill and strolled through the unchained fence to the pool. He dove into the deep end, baptizing himself in the water. He swam down toward the glowing fluorescence of the lights at the bottom of the pool. He closed his eyes and smiled, finally at peace with the world. He realized that before now, he'd never been completely clean.

Suddenly a female form broke the surface from above, diving down right in front of him. Caesar watched as Tonya sunk to the bottom, eyes squeezed shut. She grabbed hold of the drain on the bottom with her fingers and held herself there, trying to drown.

Caesar instantly propelled himself down, pried her fingers off their death grip from the drain, scooped her up and floated her to the surface, cradled in his arms. He anchored himself on the deep end ladder, letting her float in his arms. Tonya's eyes popped open as she spit pool water out and looked around in shock, before finally settling on Caesar.

"You know, all you had to say was, 'Caesar don't leave me,'" he said.

"You said from the beginning that you weren't going to let me leave. You lied," she said, in the midst of a coughing fit.

"Only an idiot doesn't change his mind," Caesar replied.

"What about your family?"

"My family just tried to drown herself," he said.

"I... I couldn't think of a happy place," she said.

"How about now?" he asked.

She looked away.

"What?" he asked.

"So what's changed? What's different now?"

He floated her closer, hugging her to him tightly.

"Up until tonight I've been in love with a fantasy that I didn't deserve, so it slipped away from me and I didn't notice," he said.

She started shivering in his arms but Caesar held her tightly and would not let her go.

"Now I'm in love with the one living person who forgave me before I knew I needed forgiveness," he said.

"Your son would've been lucky to have you as a father," she said.

Caesar let go of the ladder and fell back into the water with her until they were underwater together.

CHAPTER FIFTEEN
REDEMPTION

"That waitress reminds me of my mom," Tonya finally said.

"It's about time you cleared that up," said Caesar, "You've been staring at her since she brought us our coffees."

"She could actually be my mother," Tonya said. "Not that she'd even recognize me these days. I was a little girl when I ran away from Shady Acres that night."

Caesar looked across the table at the woman staring back at him. He had mistaken her for a girl when they first met, but he realized that she was already a hardened, stubborn, tough woman. It was only the lens that had changed.

He gazed over her head, trying to process everything that had happened.

"What?" Tonya asked.

"I was thinking about something Leo said to me once," he answered.

Caesar got quiet after that, remembering all the things Leo said to him.

"And?" she prompted.

"And that's it," he said, "I learned a lot of stuff from that guy."

"What was the most important lesson he taught you?" she asked.

"The one I'm about to act on right now," he answered, reaching across the table and grasping her hand tightly.

Tonya's eyes widened and her breath became quicker.

"Bonnie, it's time we both came clean and started over," he said.

"Both?" she said quietly.

Caesar looked into her eyes and thought he saw flickering flames.

"It's OK. I understand why you did it," he said and exhaled deeply, stirring his coffee.

Tonya was speechless, staring at him across the table, tears welling up in her bloodshot eyes.

"You and Leo and I… we all got pushed into doing some bad stuff. And some people would blame all that stuff on their circumstances. Maybe most people do. They come from shit and then do some shit. But you and I know better than that. It's not right. The stuff that's done to us is one thing. But the stuff we do because of it is a different story. There are very few things that are really beyond a person's control in life."

He paused.

"Now whatever happened at Shady Acres, as far as I'm concerned, stays there."

She nodded, looking down.

"But I only see one way out for myself," he said.

Tonya looked up at him.

"Oh no…" she started.

"See that phone over there on the wall by the restrooms?" he pointed toward the phone but Tonya kept her gaze locked on his face.

She shook her head.

"No Caesar… don't make me do it. You're a good person— now more than ever. And if I could help them see that…" she begged.

"That may be true," he said, "but that doesn't erase all the times I haven't been a good person."

"I don't want to lose you," she said.

Tears were streaking down her sunburned cheeks.

"This is the only way you won't lose me," he said. "This is the only way we can start over, clean."

She started to protest again but he stopped her.

"And you know it, you know it in your heart Tonya. Your heart is the thing that has been guiding us this whole time. It's how we kept finding each other, over and over. It's the thing that saved me," Caesar said.

She leaned over the table and kissed him, knowing in that same heart that it would be a long time if forever before she would be with him again.

"You'll make the call?" he asked when their lips parted.

"I will," she said.

She looked at him one last time before grabbing her things and walking quickly toward the restrooms and the phone. By the time she had picked up the receiver, dialed 9-1, and looked back at their booth, it was empty. Except for a set of dog tags in the center of the table.

She looked out the large diner windows and spotted him out in the parking lot, just as he disappeared behind an 18-wheeler. And then Caesar was gone. Tonya dialed the final number and kept her promise.

CHAPTER SIXTEEN
PREACHER MAN

"Hey preacher, wrap it up so we can get to chow on time!" an inmate yelled from the back of the chapel.

Standing at the prison chapel pulpit in navy blue prison clothes, a big pewter cross on a rope around his neck and a silver wedding band on his finger, Caesar read three more complete bible passages out loud before remembering that he was the target of the inmate shouting. His one time peers weren't about to let him off the hook.

"Jesus don't like you any more than the rest of us!" one yelled.

Caesar looked over at the prison guards lining the room. They smirked and whispered amongst themselves, making no attempt to quiet the rowdy inmates sitting in folding chairs in front of Caesar's pulpit. And he didn't expect them to either.

Not enough time had yet passed between when, thanks to Tonya's diner phone call, they finally hauled him back to his rightful place in prison to serve out the rest of his life. He didn't even protest when the judge pinned Leo's murder on him, not believing Caesar's defense that the clerk had done it. Although he hadn't physically pulled the trigger, Caesar felt more responsible for Leo's death than anyone else possibly could. So he took the rap and accepted that the only legitimate way to clear up his soul, as he had told Tonya was absolutely necessary, was to spend the rest of his life behind bars.

As his new wife she wasn't overjoyed by this news, but she understood him enough to know that there wasn't any other way for him to live with himself, and mainly, to fully repent for the death of his practice son, and in a way, his real son.

From the beginning the guards put Caesar on the same level as cop killers and pedophiles, not particularly caring that he hadn't committed either of those crimes. The other prisoners treated him like a prison snitch. These two things would have enraged the old Caesar, triggering thoughts of revenge. He would have thought it unfair and lashed out at the world. But his old self was so blind that he didn't recognize his own hand in front of his face.

The re-born Caesar understood why he was being treated this way and knew that he deserved every bit of it. He knew it was part of his penance and even welcomed the abuse that came with it.

When he befriended the prison chaplain, molding himself in his image and clearing up all his jumbled confusions about the Lord, guards and inmates alike naturally assumed that Caesar was a deplorable, boot-licking brown-noser. Caesar didn't bother to set them straight. He had learned from the chaplain how a lot of people had the wrong idea about Jesus and he didn't try to set them straight either. They either believed him or they didn't. This gave Caesar a deep, overwhelming sense of inner peace that all the bullets in the world had never been able to do.

He was overjoyed when the chaplain made him a junior prisoner chaplain and let him lead his own services in the prison chapel. Even as the guards joked and the inmates jeered, Caesar felt his purpose shine through because there was always that one guy in the back of the chapel. His face, and sometimes the color of his skin changed over time, but he was always there. Through the choruses of catcalls and chaos, he would look up at Caesar in the pulpit with an innocent curiosity (or as much innocence as a prisoner could realistically possess). Caesar knew that, over and over, he was looking into the face of Leo.

With the regular chaplain's help, Caesar was finally able to get through the closing prayer and end the service. When he got back to his solitary cell, a single piece of mail was lying on his bed. He admired Tonya's dainty scrawling on the envelope for a moment before opening it. When he did carefully tear a slit in the top and slide the letter out, a photo preceded it, fluttering to the floor and landing face down on the concrete. There was writing on the back that Caesar couldn't read from his seat on the bed.

A feeling of panic invaded his inner peace and overcame him. He trapped the photo under the sole of his shoe and pushed it further away. Caesar sat on his bed staring at the folded letter lying next to him and the photo trapped under his shoe.

He finally realized that even if the photo showed what he was sure it would, life would go on. Caesar finally lifted his foot and picked up the photo. He read the back first.

Tonya had simply scribbled, "Everything's going to be okay."

He flipped the photo over. All the breath in his body caught in Caesar's throat and his heart felt like it would surely explode. The belly in this photo was smaller than in the tattered photo he had carried around all those years before. This flat belly had a tattoo of an angel encircling the navel.

Inside the letter, Tonya had scrawled the words to a new song:

"The first belly was for her.

This one is for us.

The first made you want to run.

This one will make you stay.

The first turned out to be her last.

This one is only the beginning.

The first absorbed his father's sins.

This one will be born to a saint.

The first belly lived only in a photo.

This belly is real.

This love is real.

This time is real."

EPILOGUE

Prison guards accompanied elderly Caesar, in his worn minister's clothing, down the center aisle of his old cellblock. Carrying a worn bible, he smiled and nodded at various other inmates as he passed them ("hey Caesar," "how's it hangin' preacher?"). At the end of the row, he stood in front of his and Leo's old cell.

"Open 13!" shouted the guard.

The doors slid open and Caesar entered, sitting in a chair facing the bottom bunk bed. He opened his bible and started flipping through it.

"Close 13!"

The doors shut and Caesar looked up at the prisoner sitting in front of him.

"So... where did we leave off?" asked Caesar.

A shadowy figure sat up in the bed and faced Caesar. The man was also old. He was bearded and his hair hung around his shoulders.

"Corinthians," he told Caesar in a feeble, quiet voice. "What no one ever saw or heard, what no one ever thought could happen, is the very thing God prepared for those who love him," the man said.

"That's right Leo," said Caesar.

CAESAR'S COMMANDMENTS

Commandment Number One:
Do the job one hundred percent or don't bother doing it at all.

Commandment Number Two:
Never swear in front of kids.

Commandment Number Three:
Once you make your choice and commit to it, never go back.

Commandment Number Four:
If someone is looking for you left, then go right.

Commandment Number Five:
Why should some other dummy know more about something than you do?

Commandment Number Six:
Never surprise a sleeping man. It's the easiest way to get yourself killed.

Commandment Number Seven:
Thou shalt not kill (unless absolutely necessary).

Commandment Number Eight:
Never lose focus.

Commandment Number Nine:
When working in groups, only one person can and should do all the thinking. Everyone else should follow.

Commandment Number Ten:
Never go back to the scene of a crime, especially your own.

Commandment Number Eleven:

Have a damn good reason for everything you do and say.

Commandment Number Twelve:

Never drop your gun. Might as well chop off your nuts.